CHINCHILLA COLORING BOOK

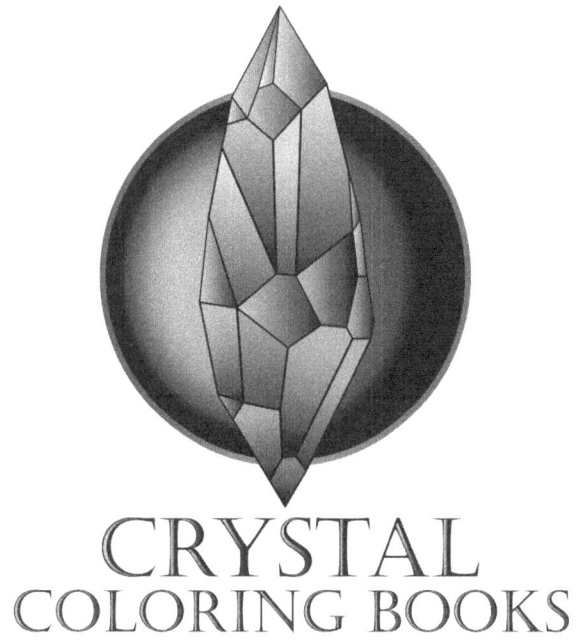

CRYSTAL COLORING BOOKS

Copyright © 2017 Crystal Coloring Books
All rights reserved.
ISBN-13: 978-1725929890
ISBN-10: 1725929899

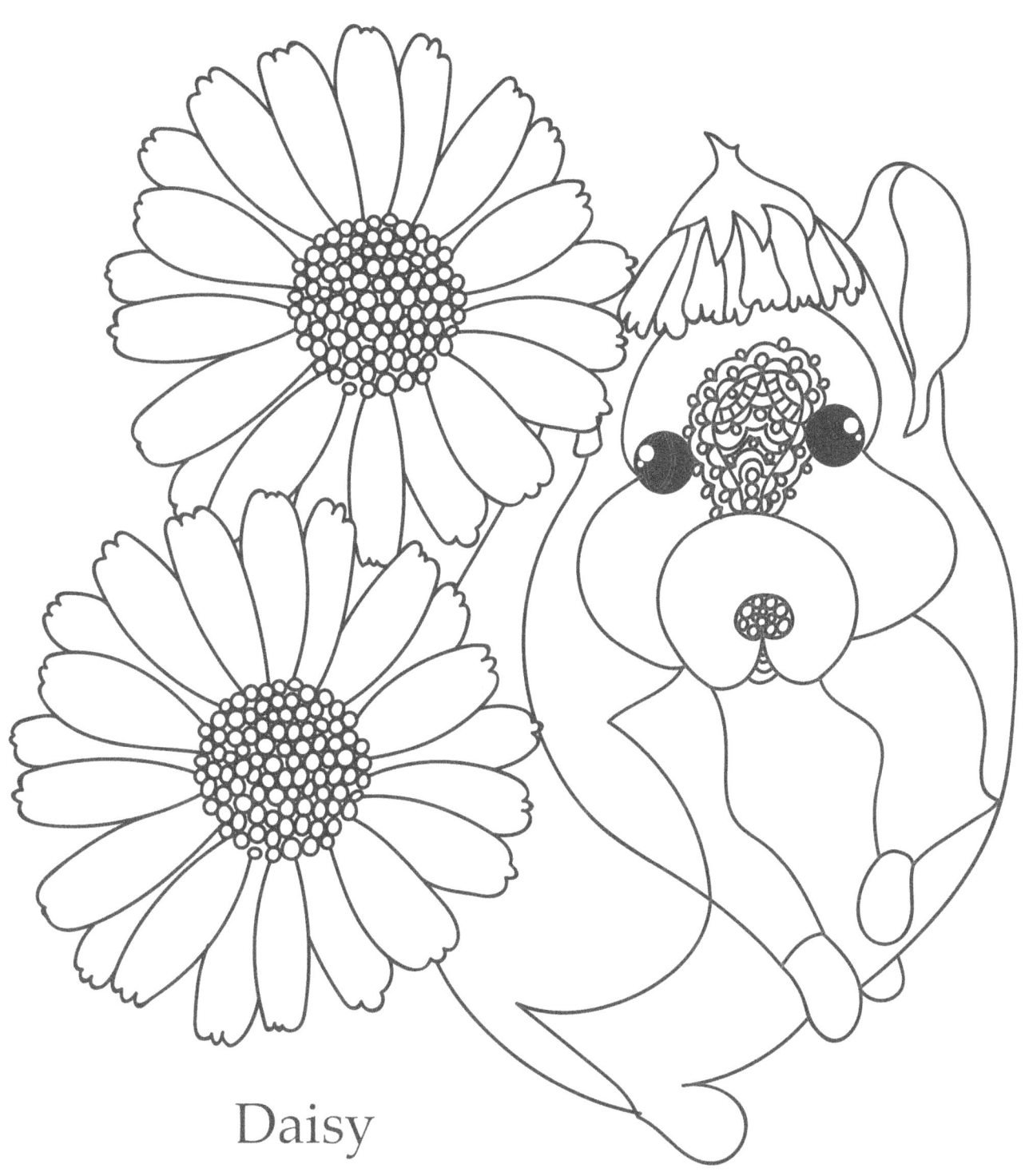

Daisy

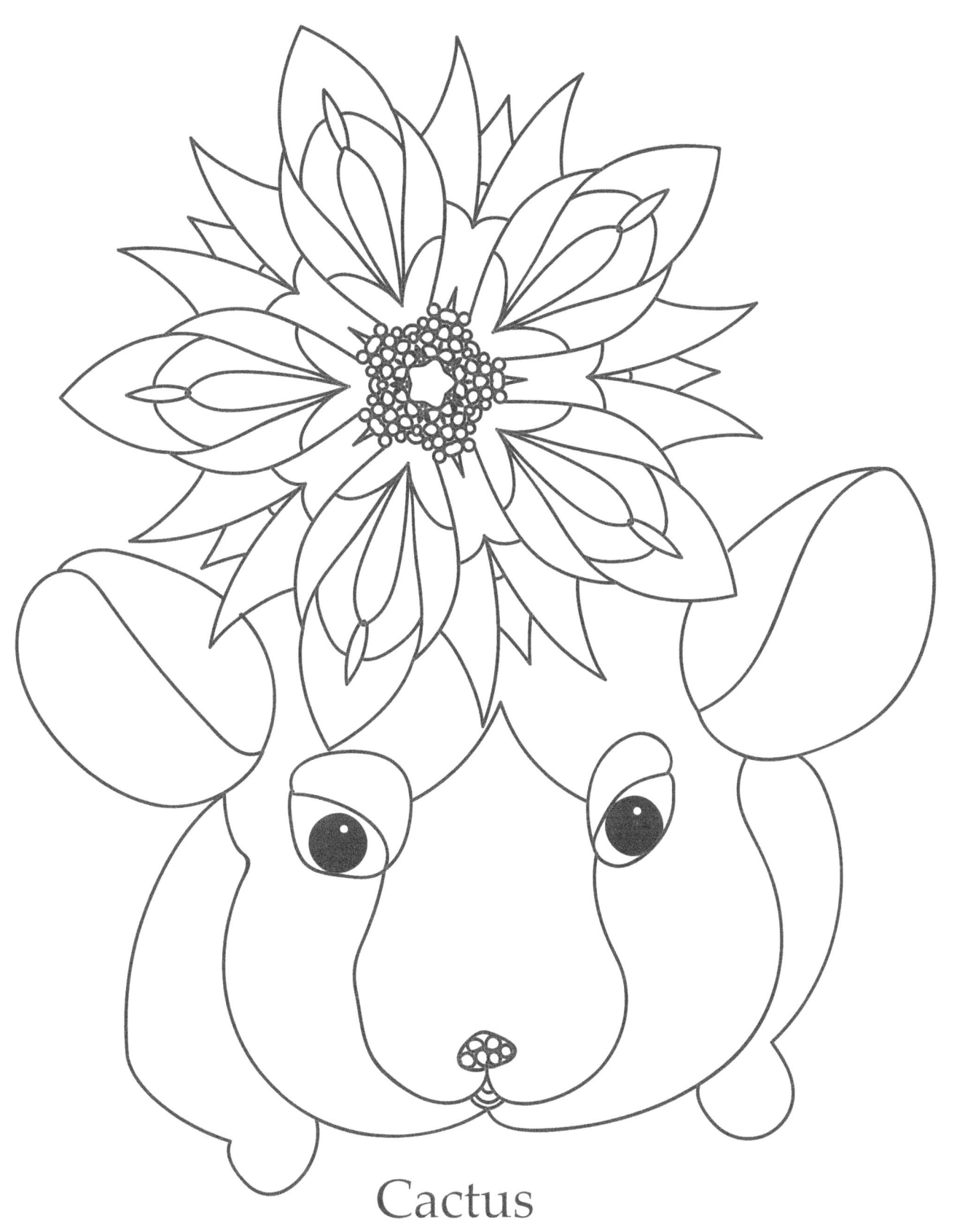
Cactus

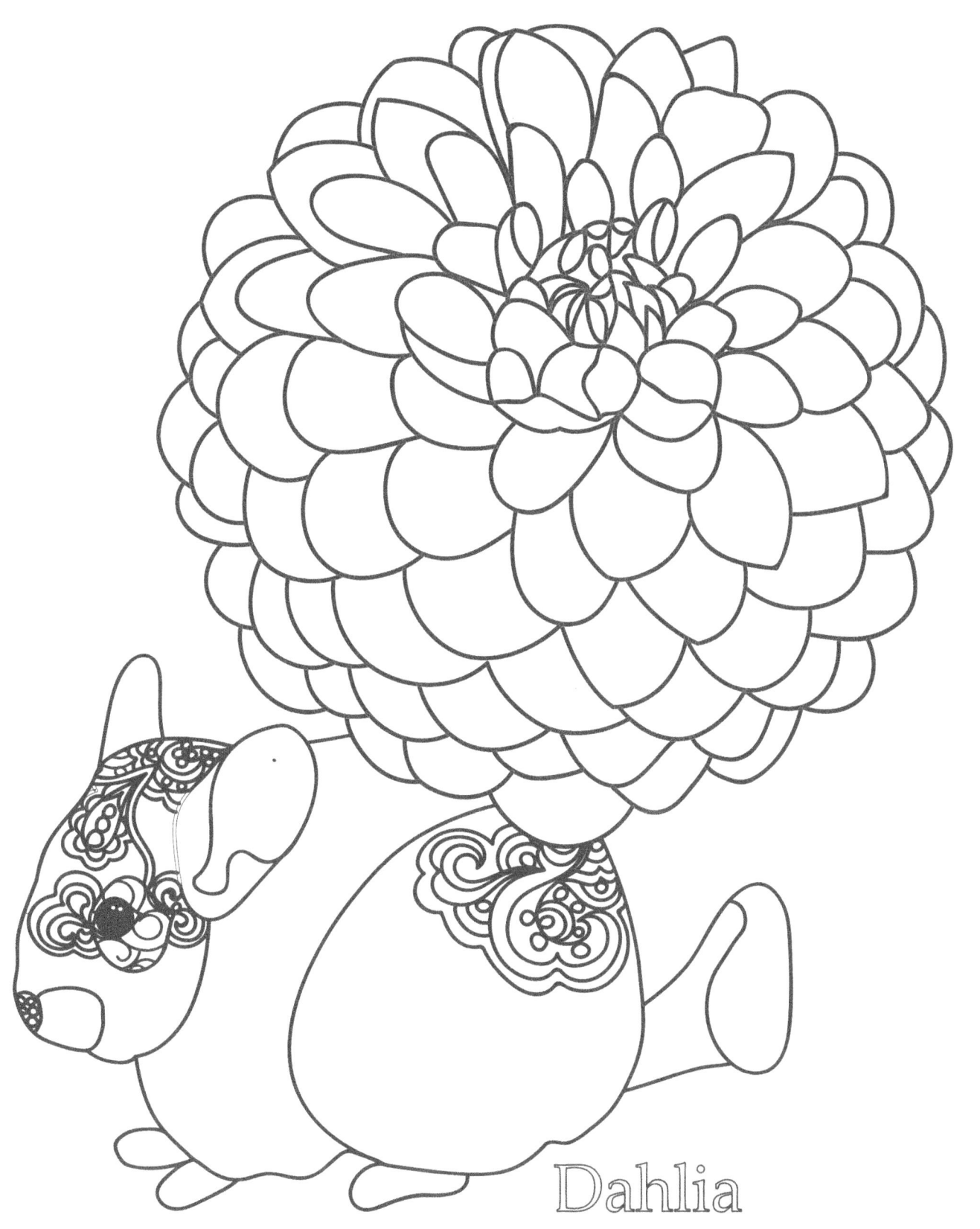

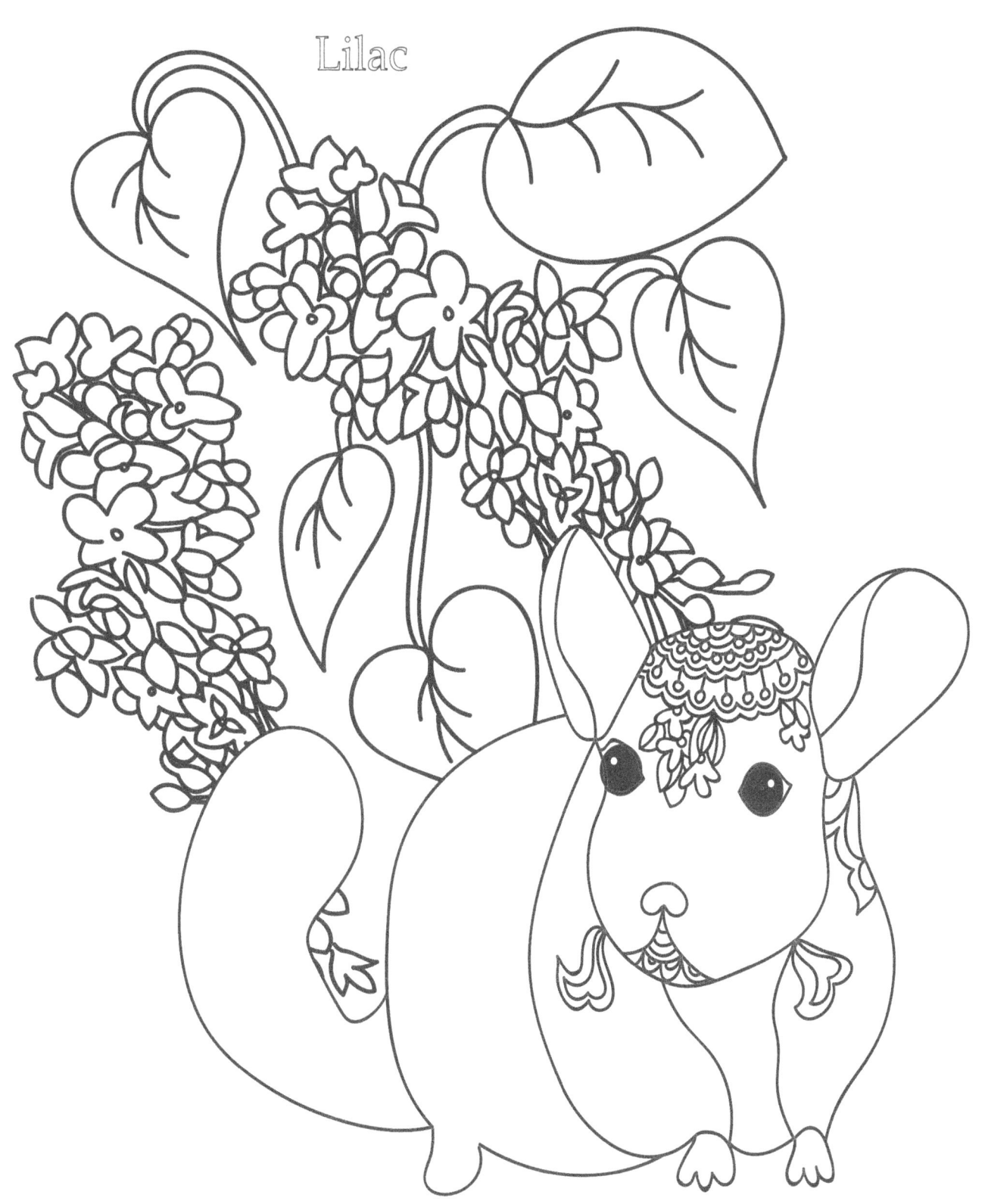

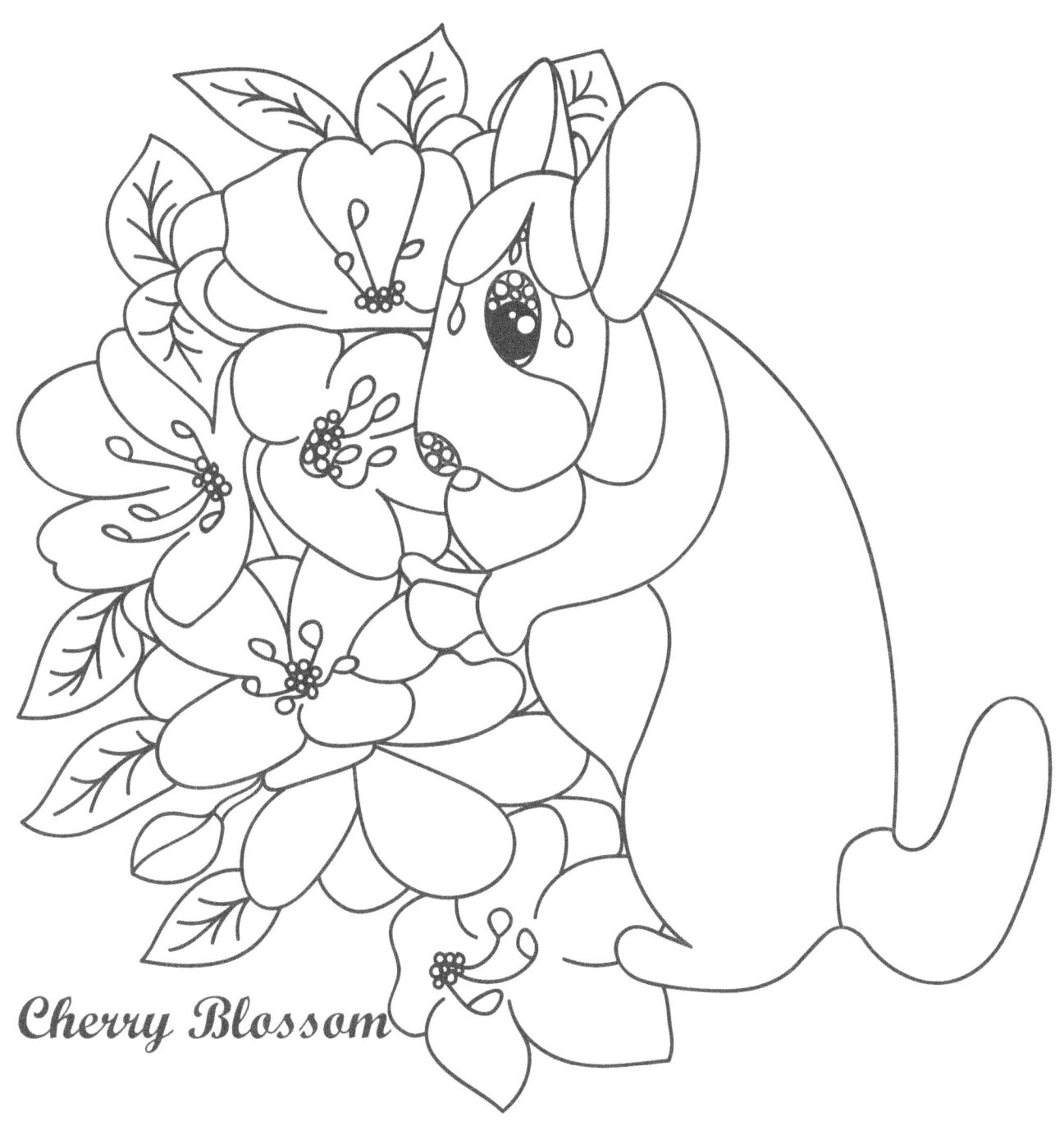

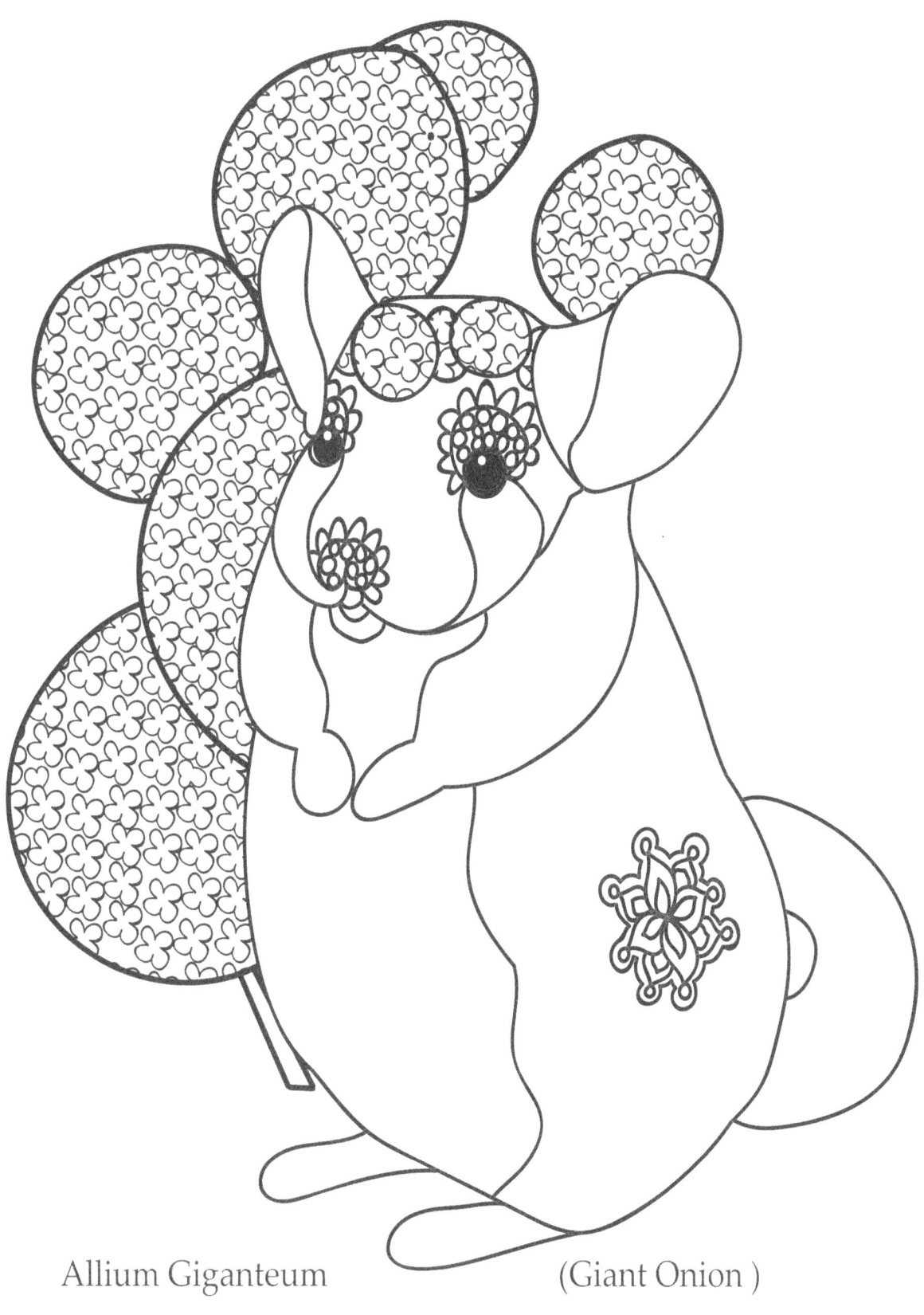

Allium Giganteum (Giant Onion)

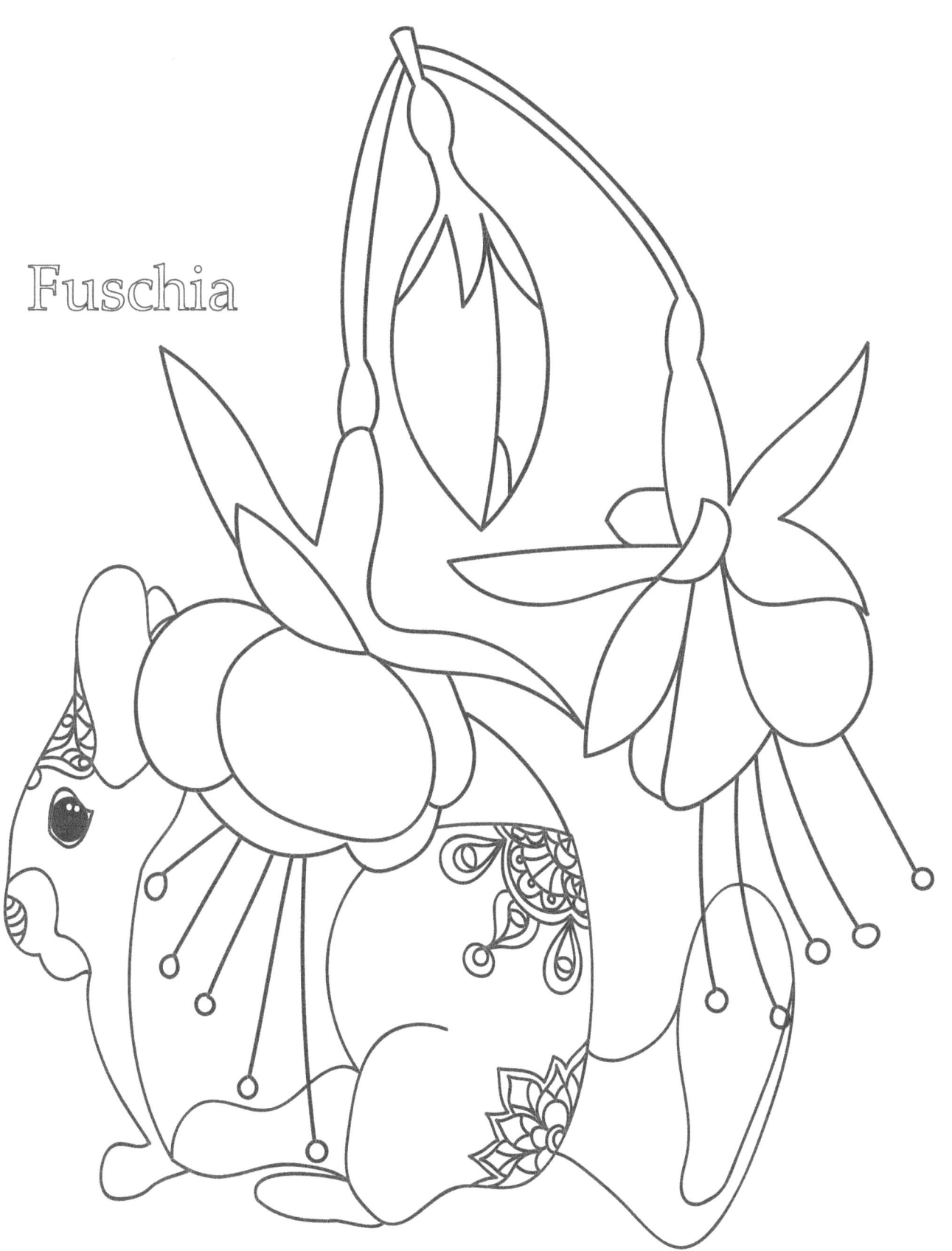
Fuschia

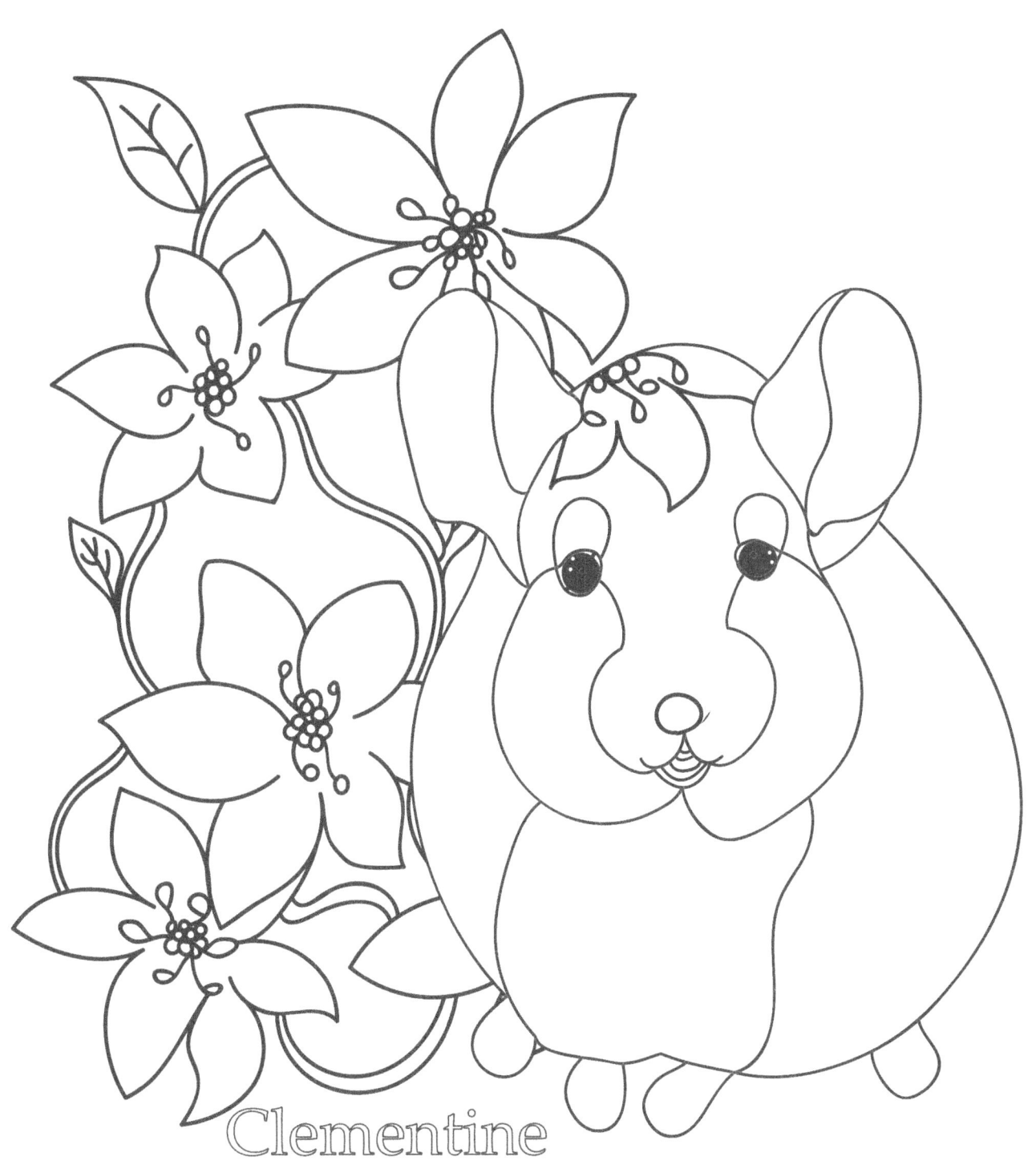

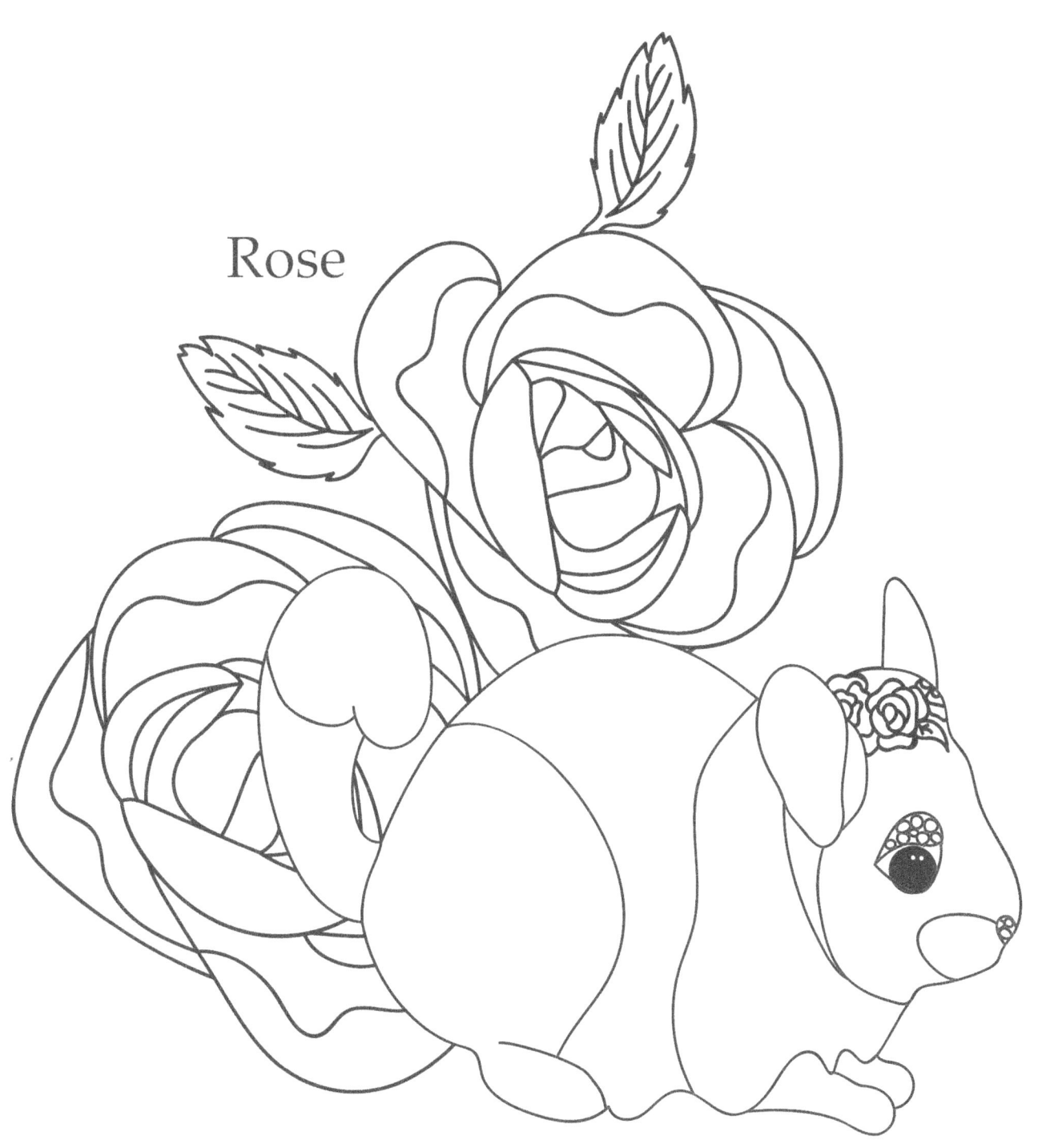

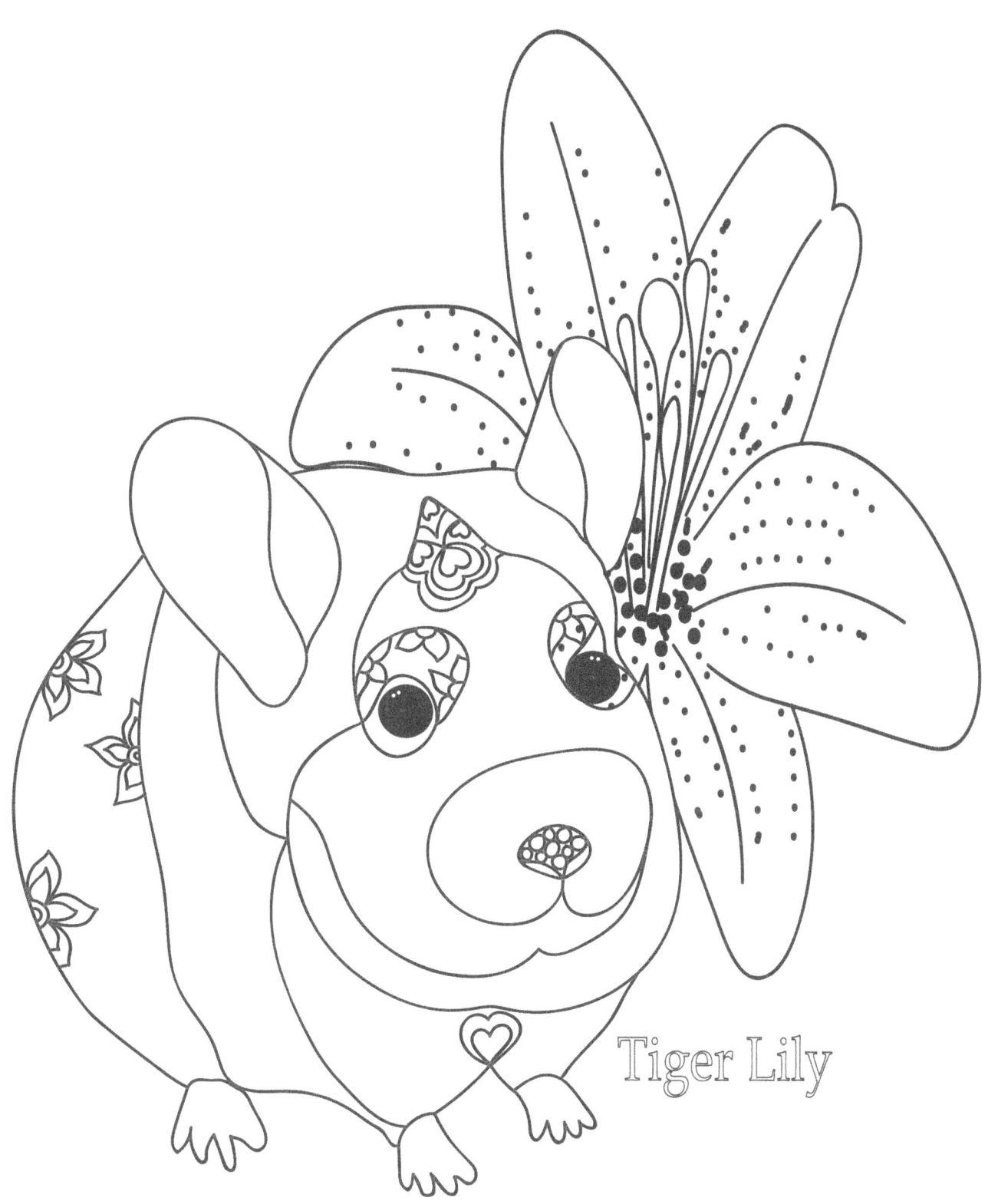

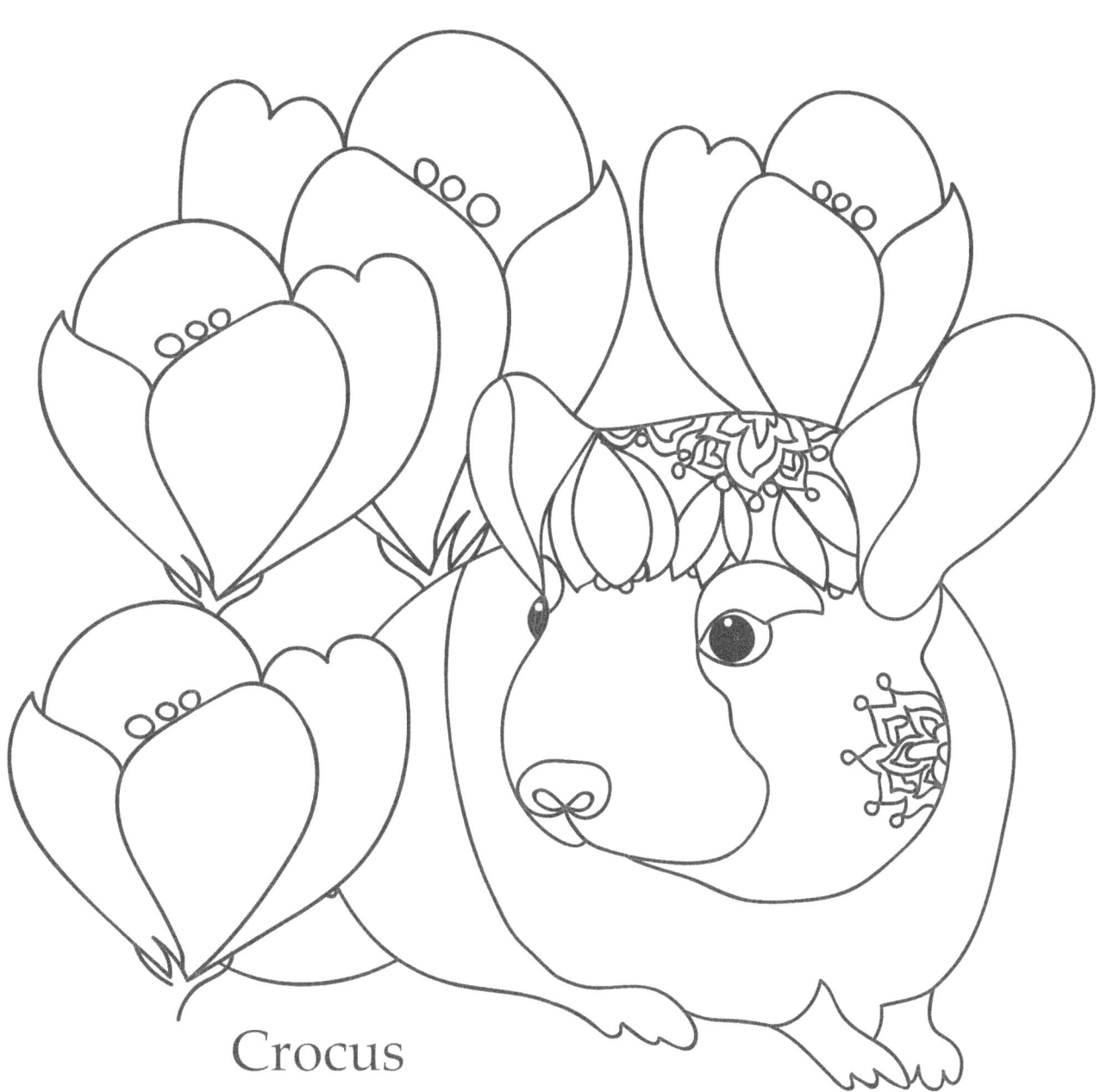
Crocus

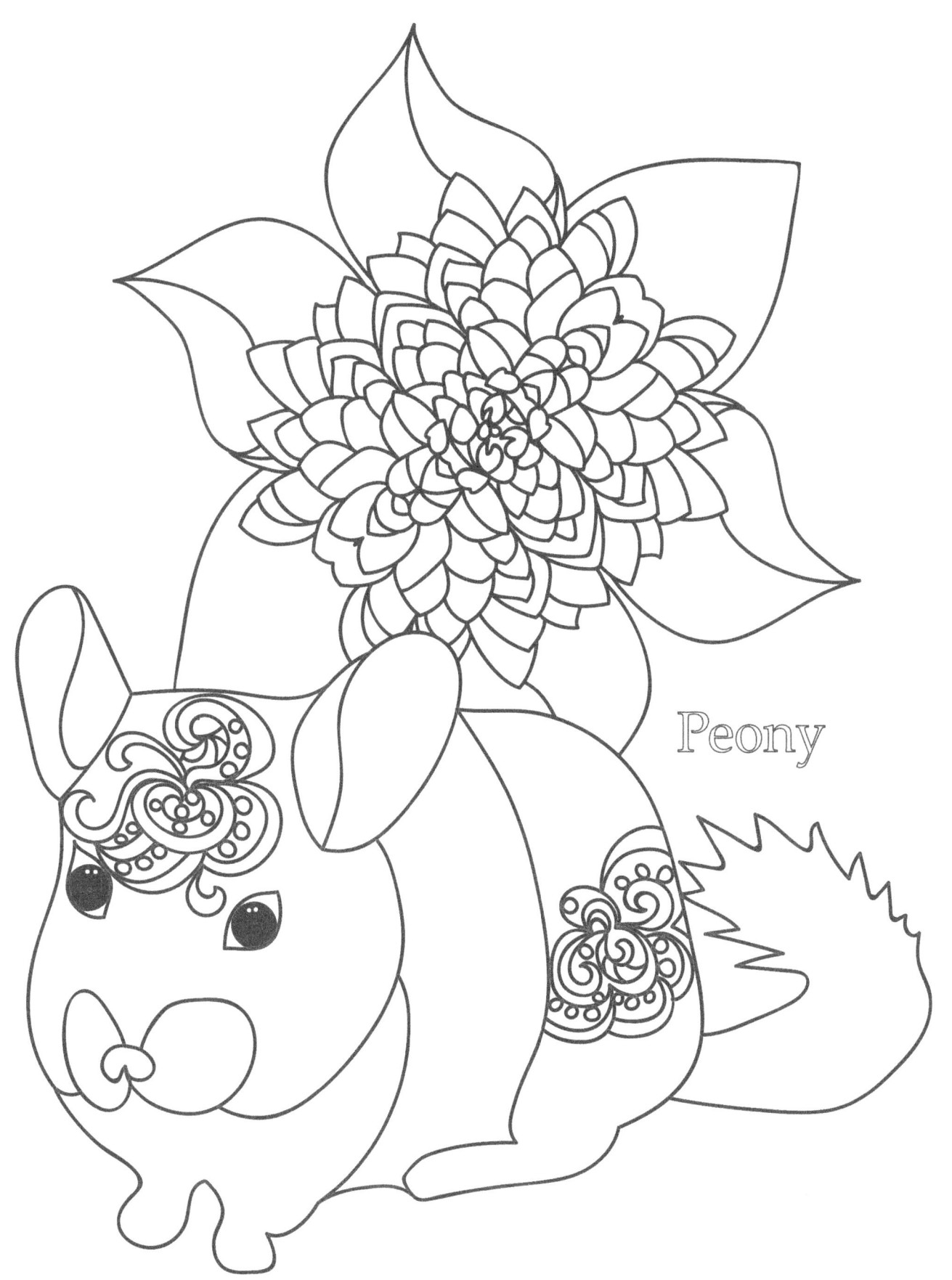

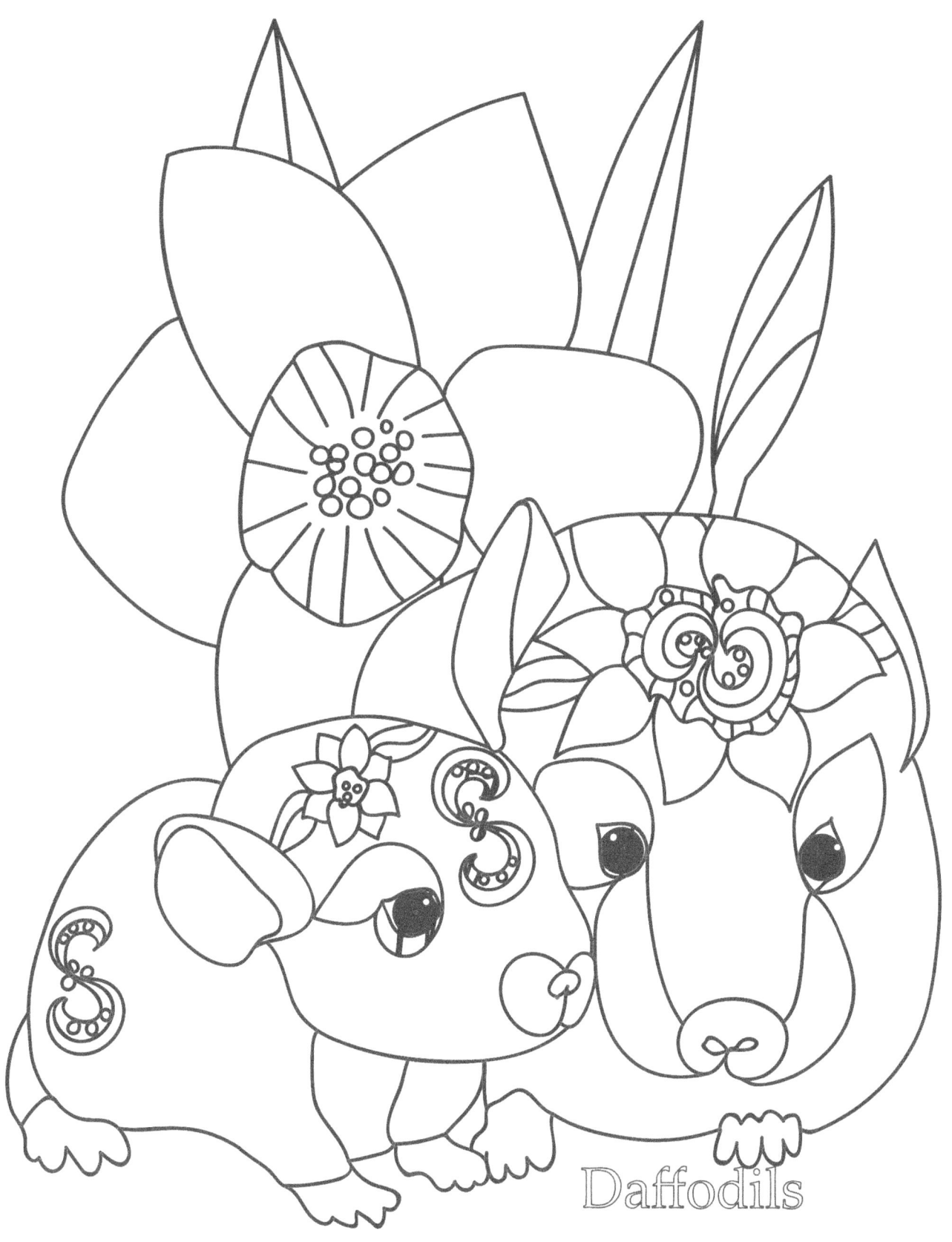

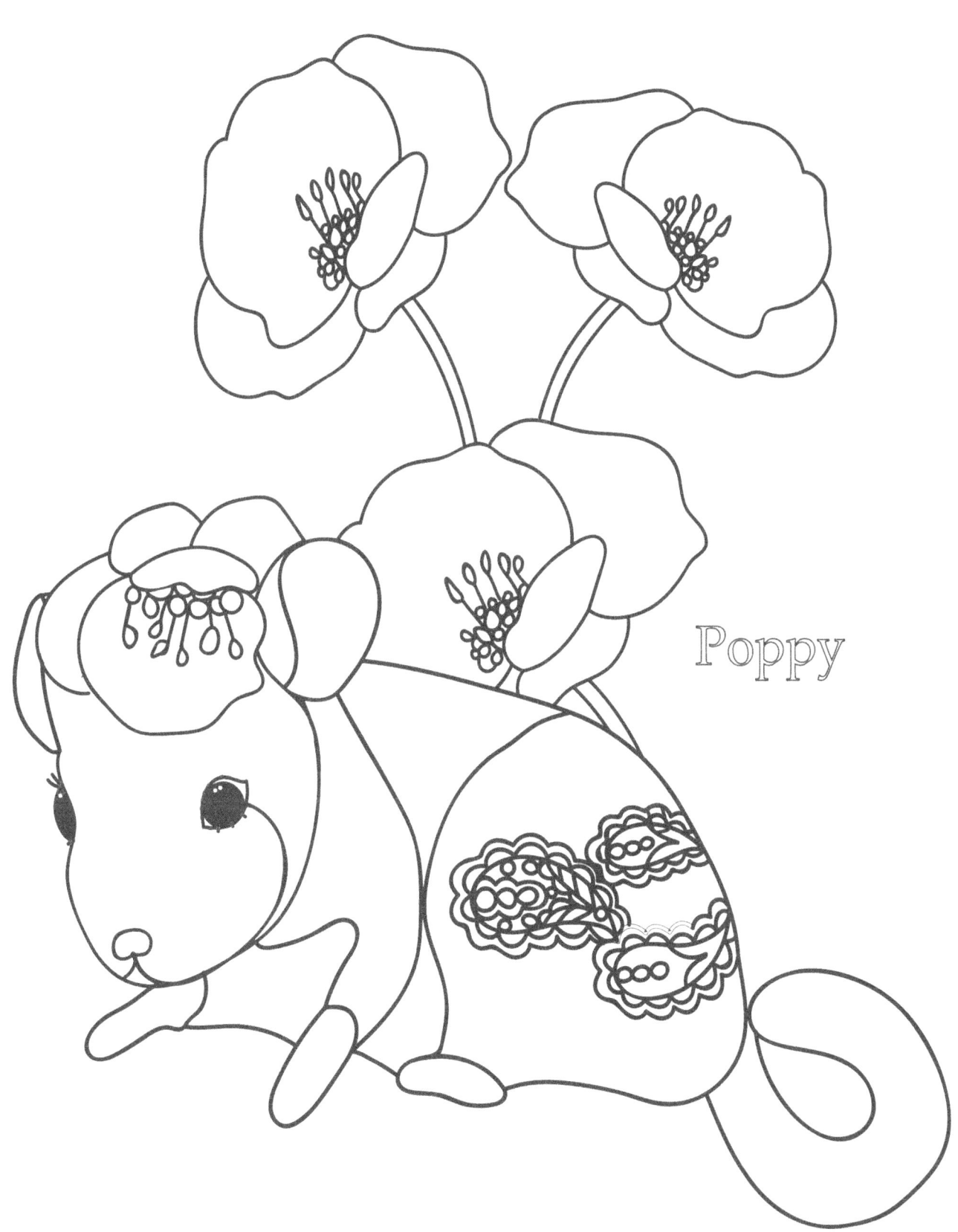
Poppy

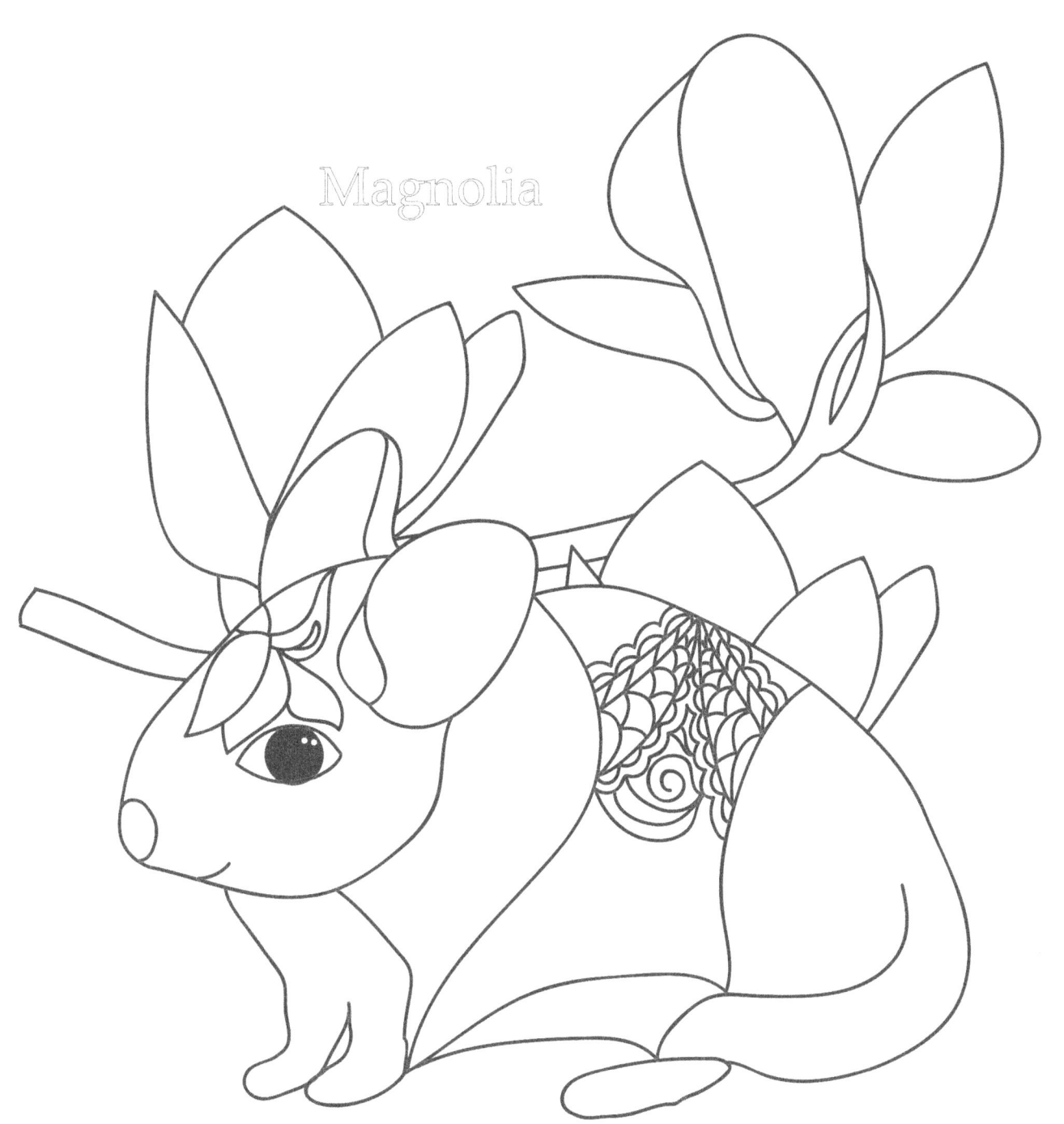

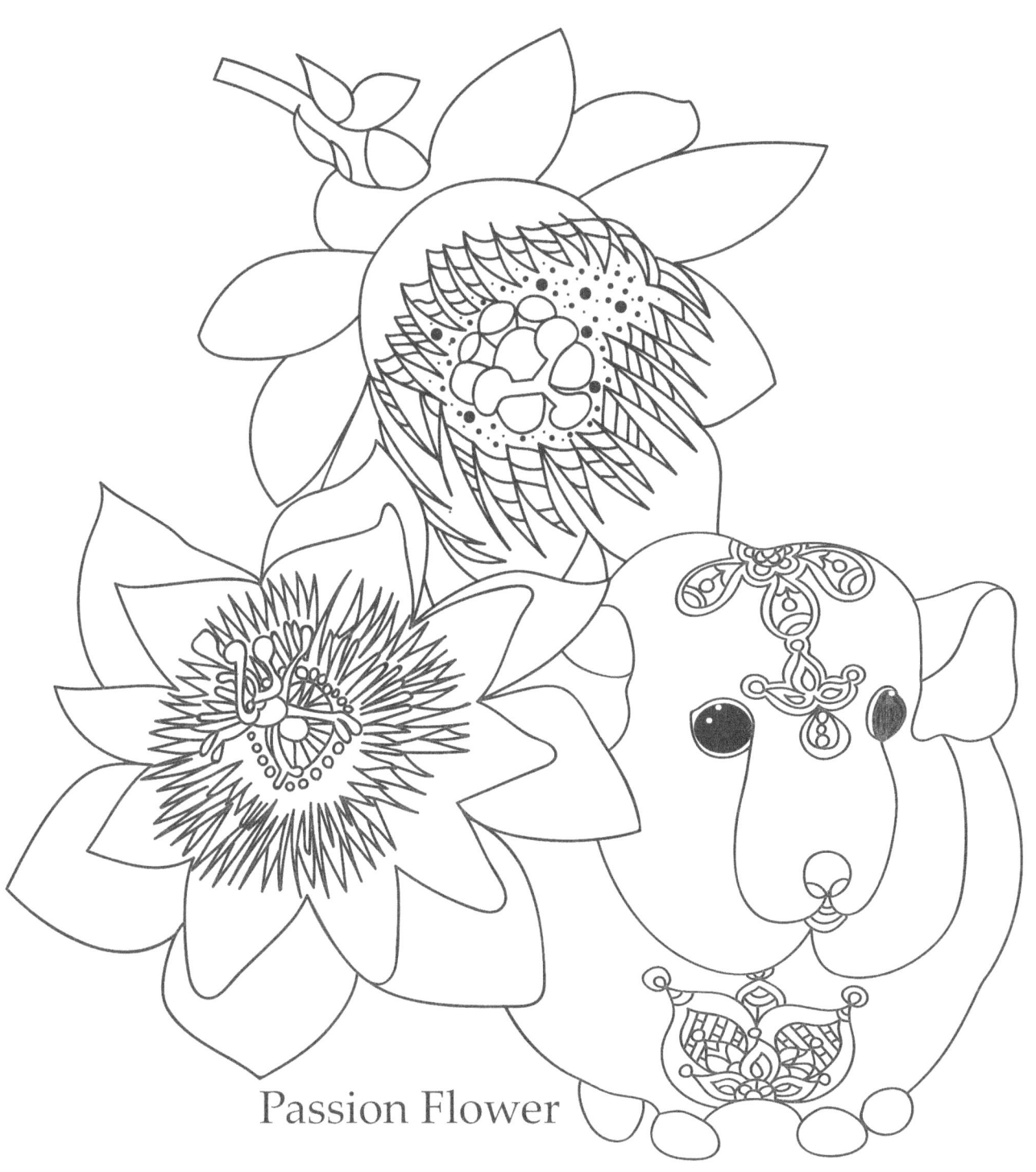
Passion Flower

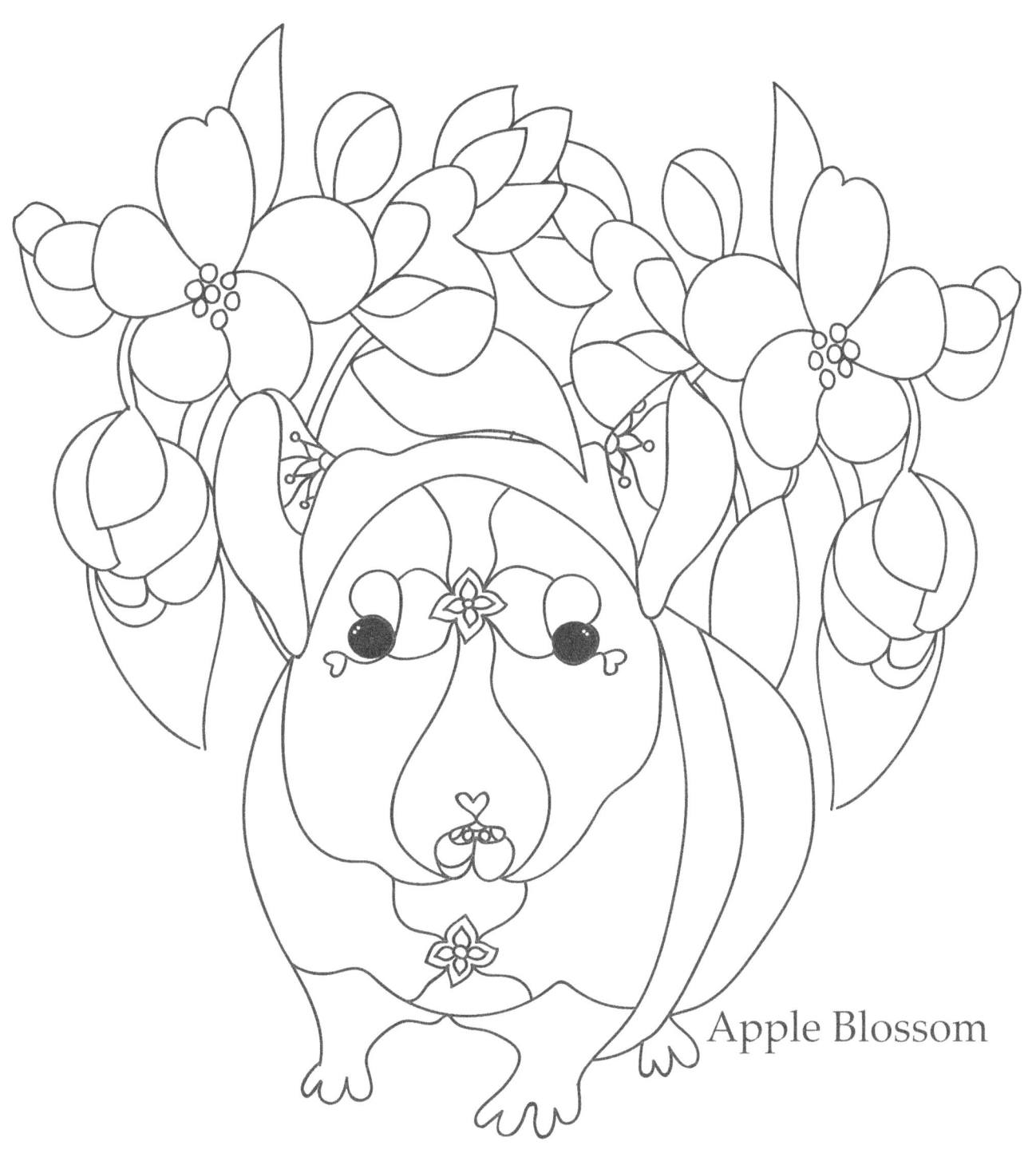

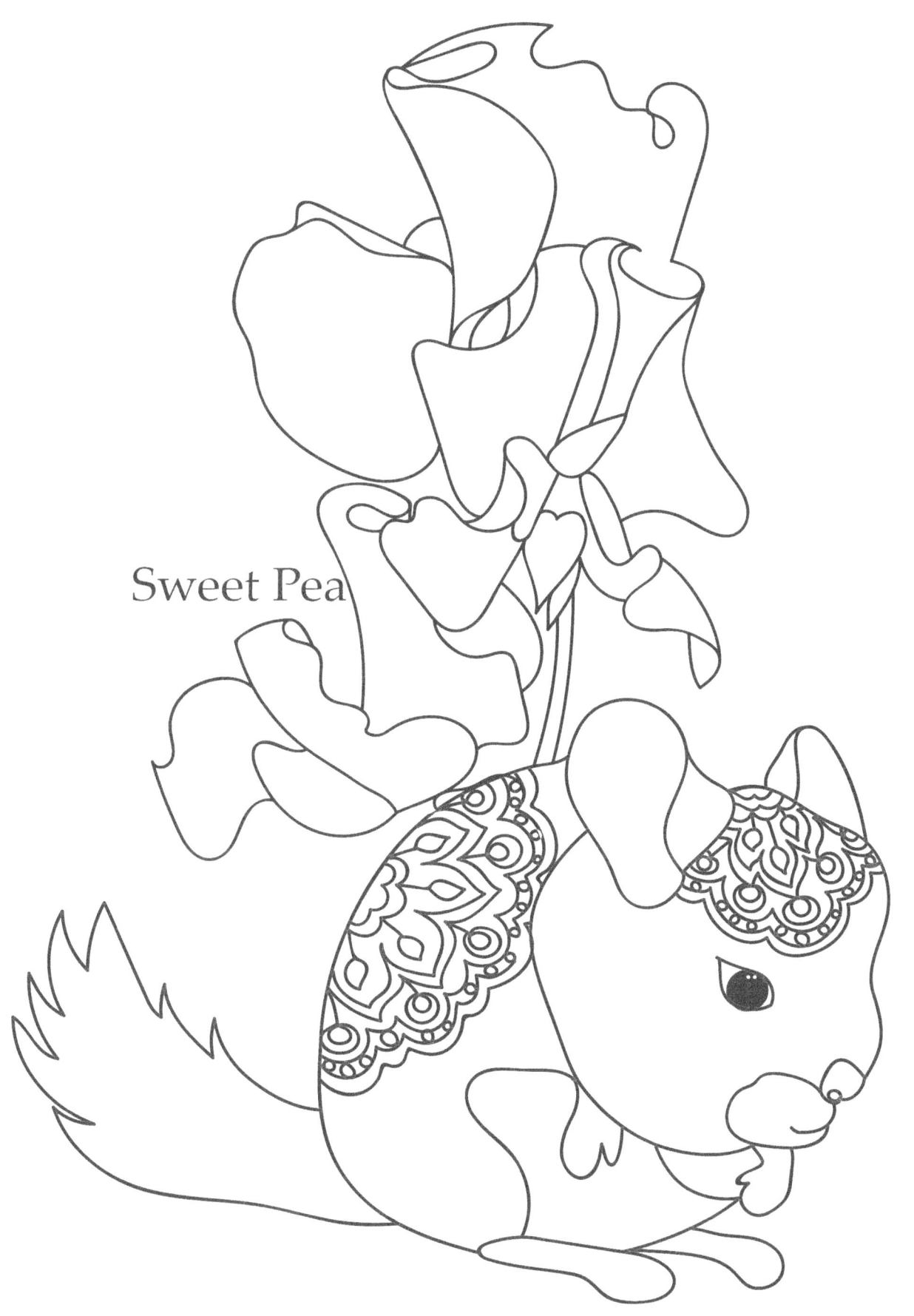
Sweet Pea

Agapanthus (Blue Lily)

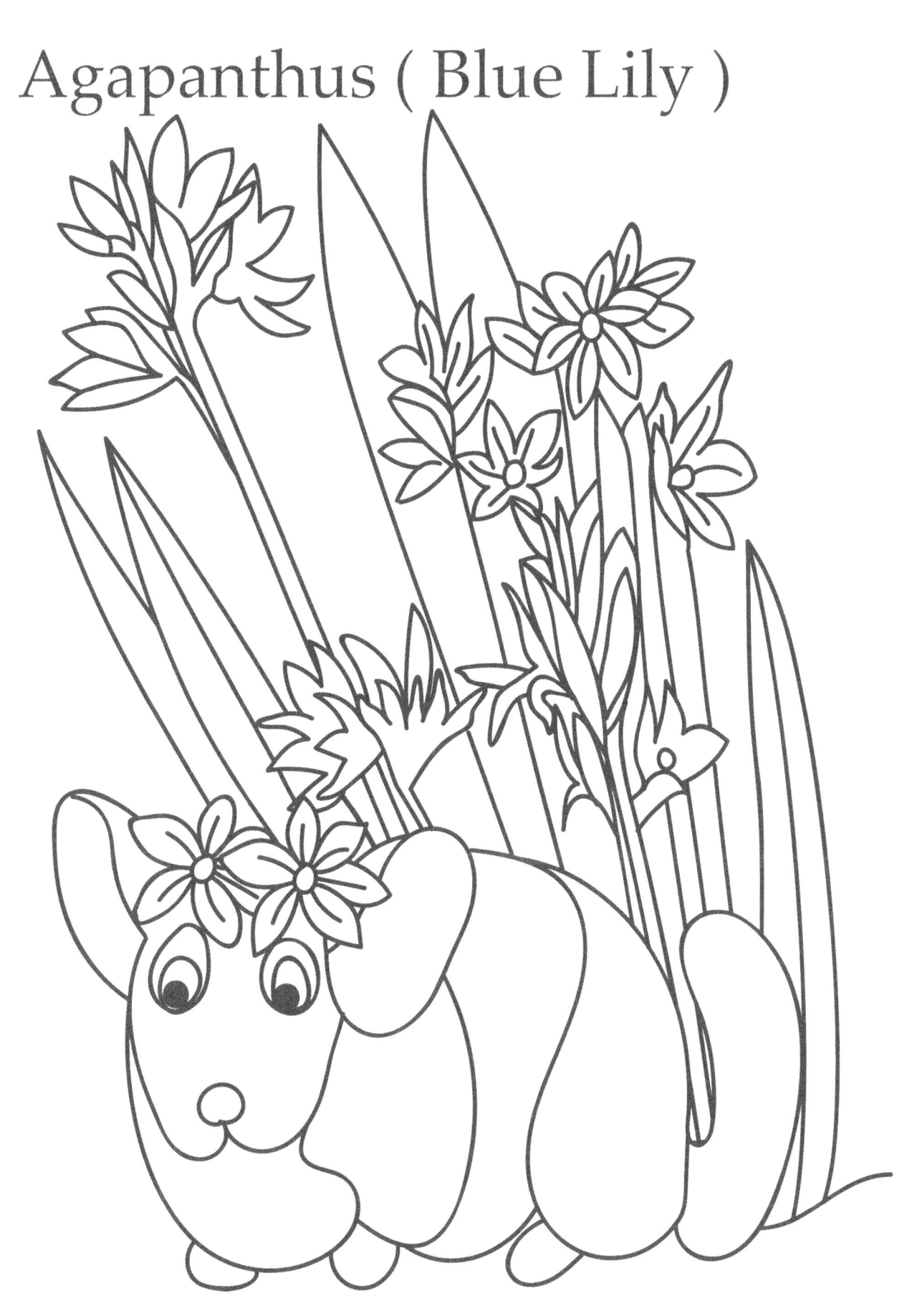

Pansy

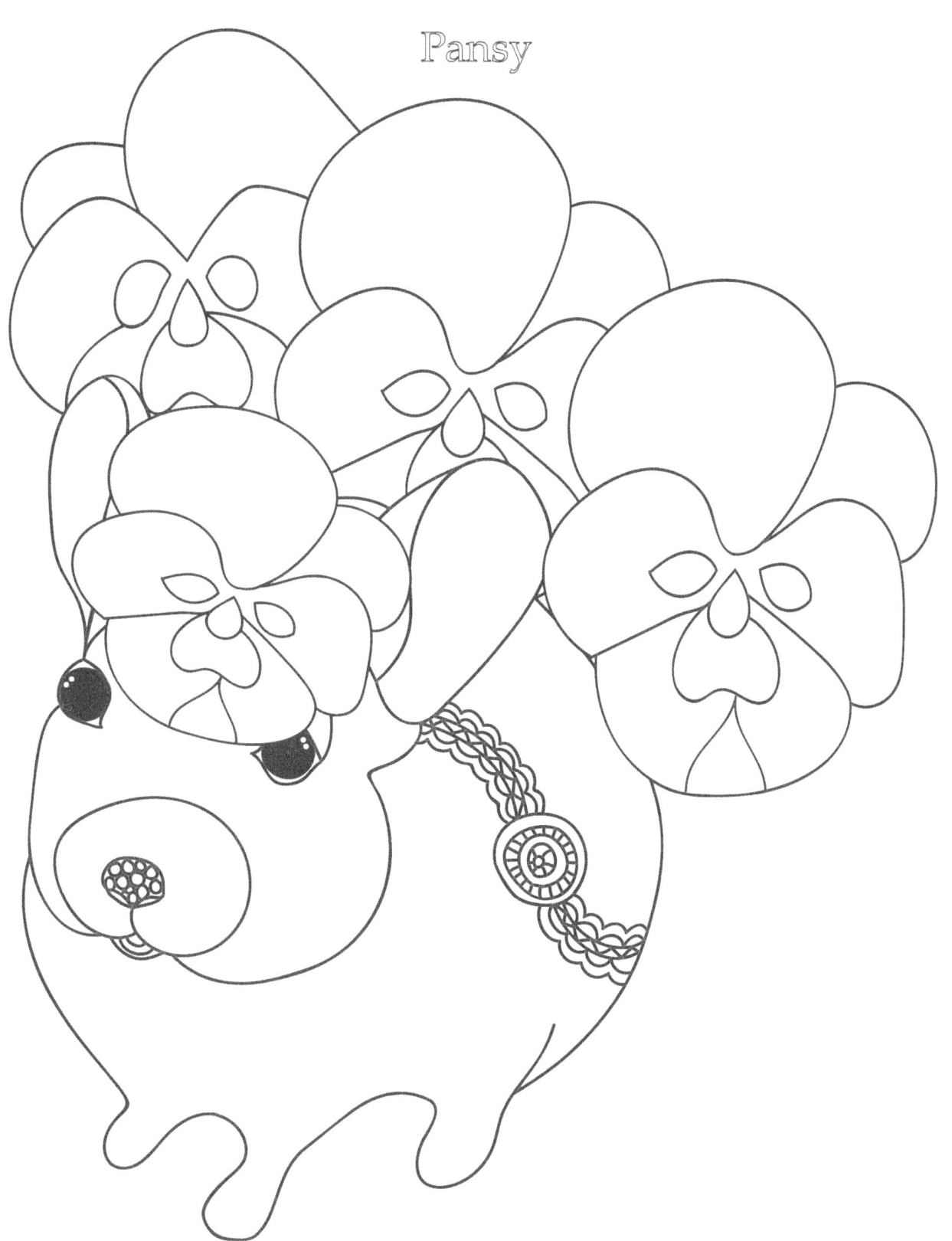

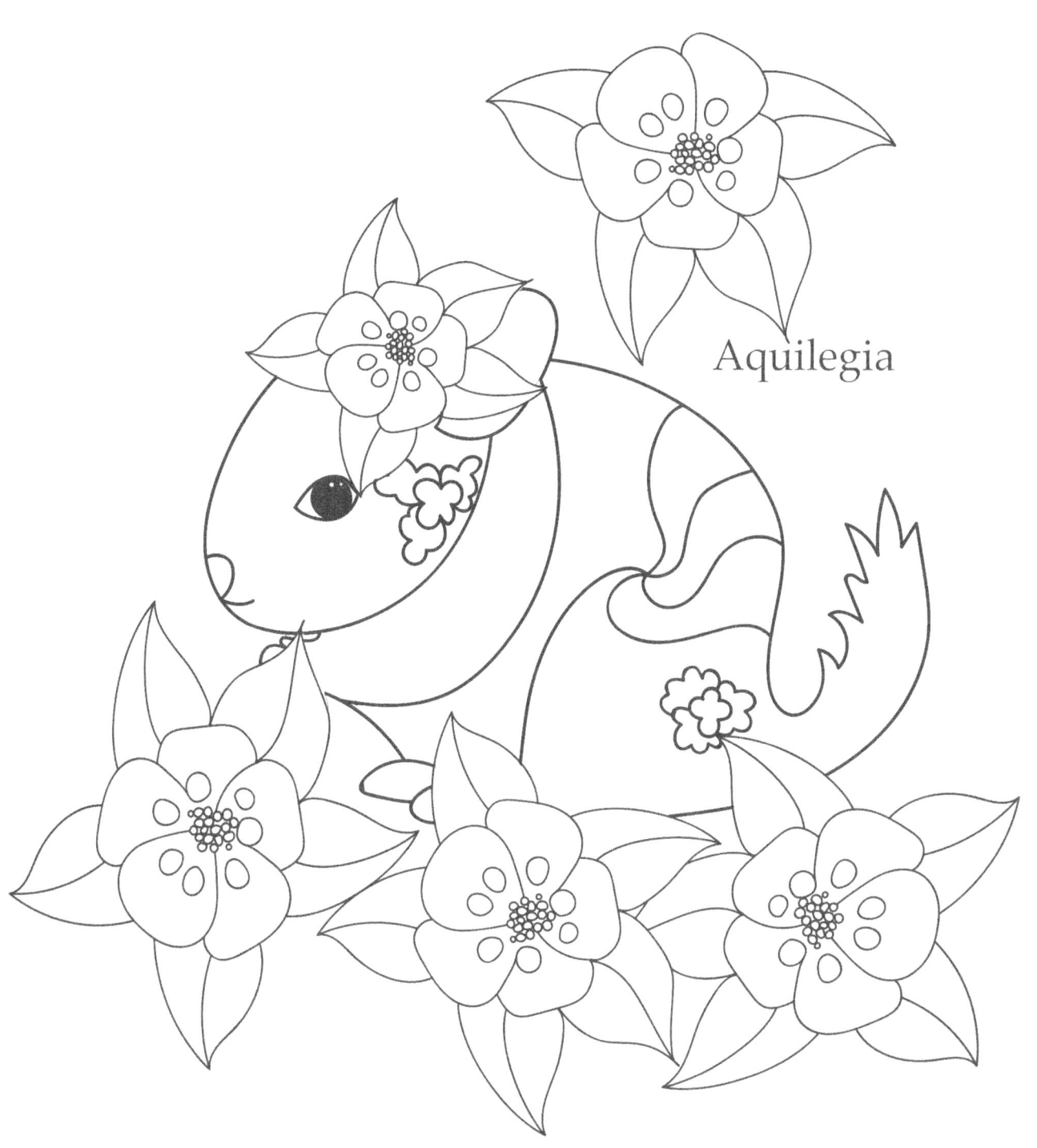

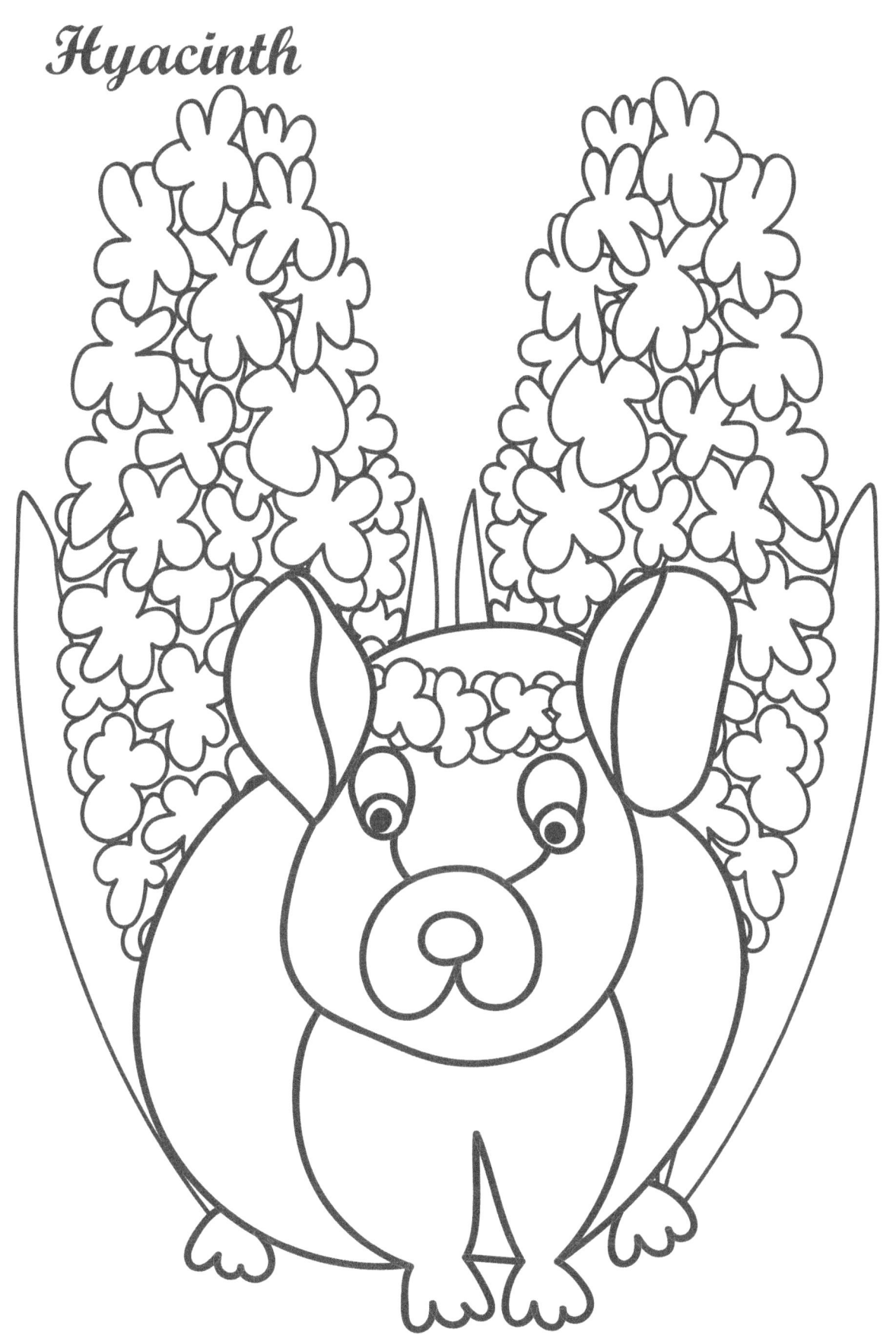

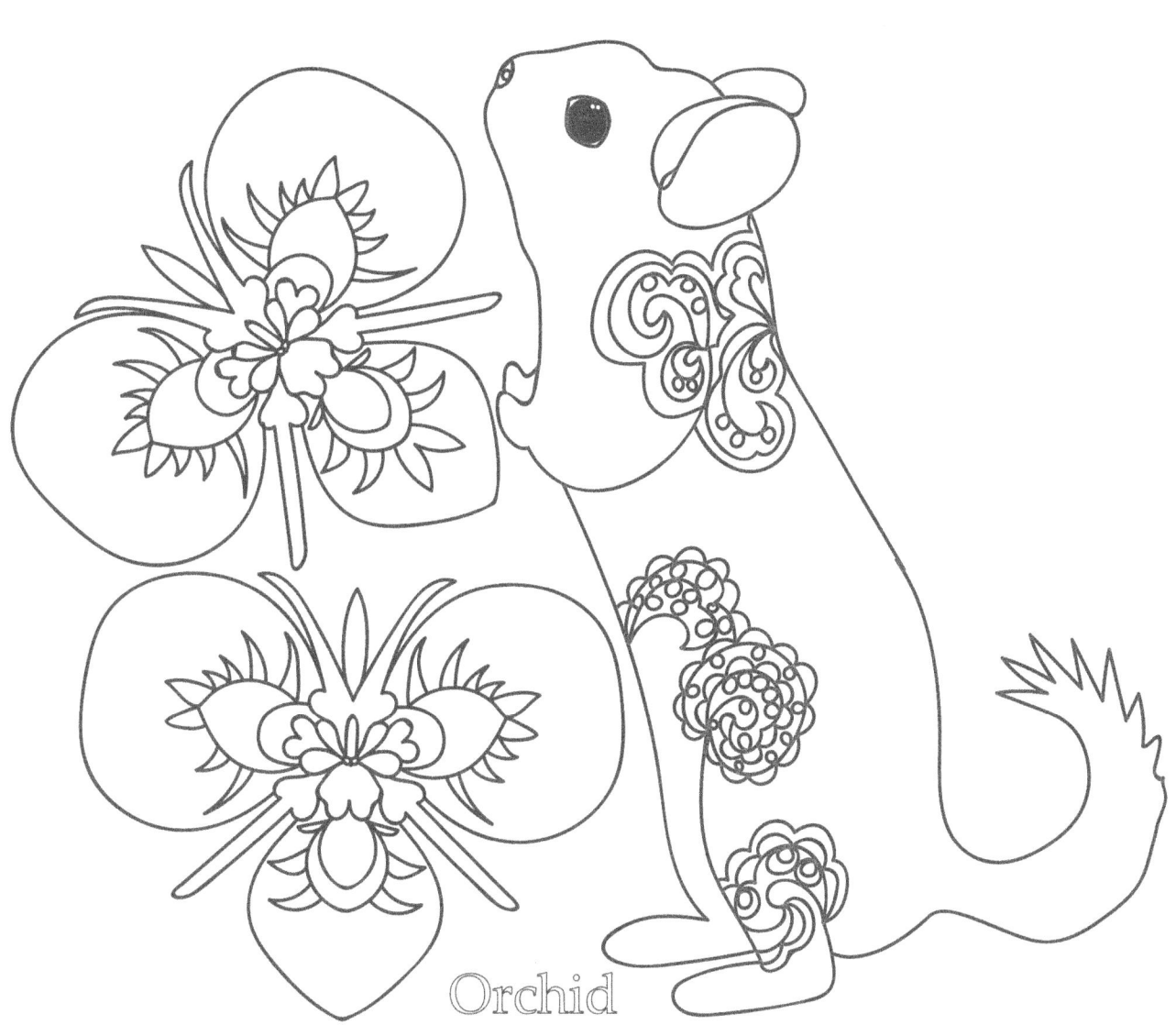

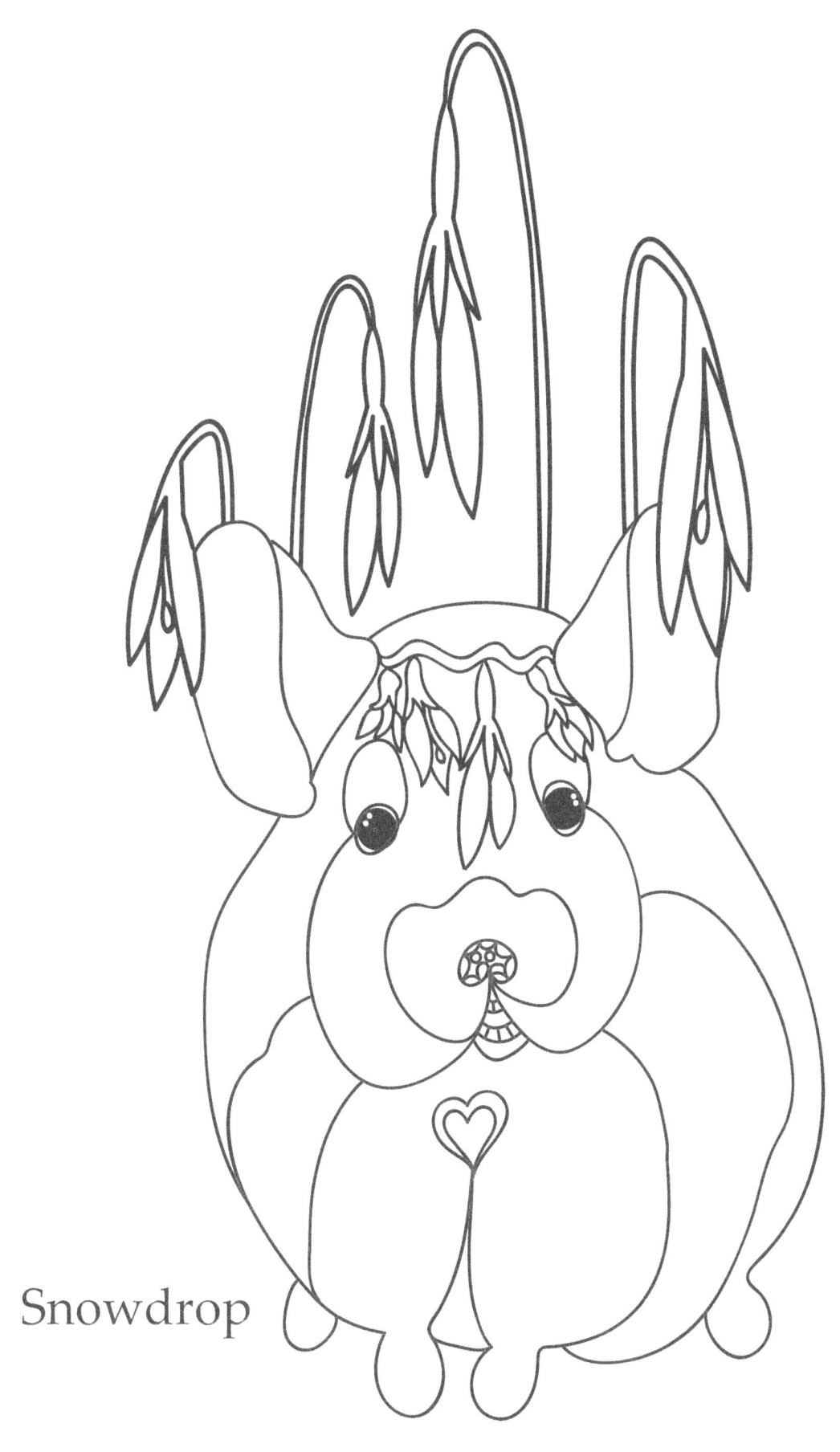

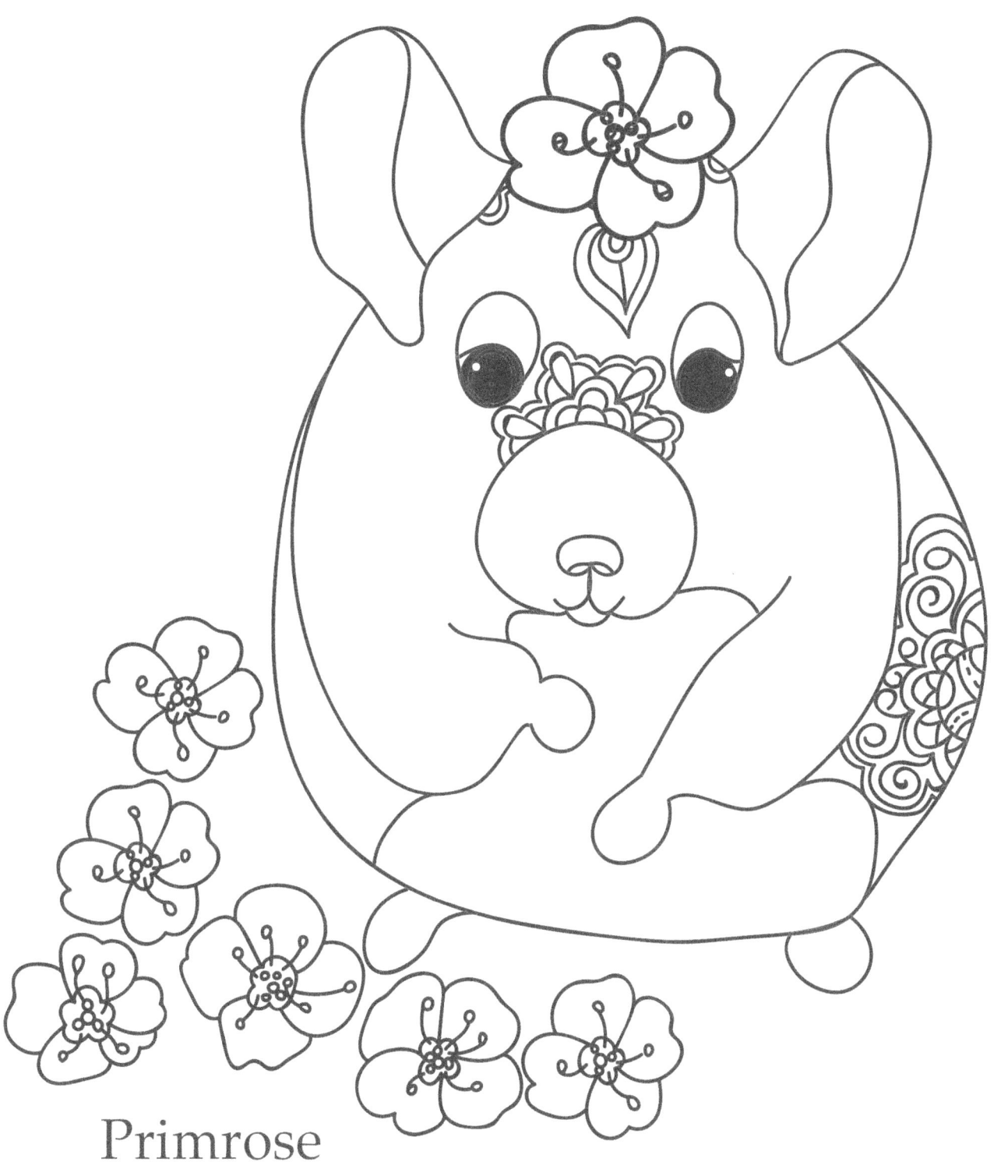
Primrose

Muscari Armeniacum
(Grape Hyacinth)

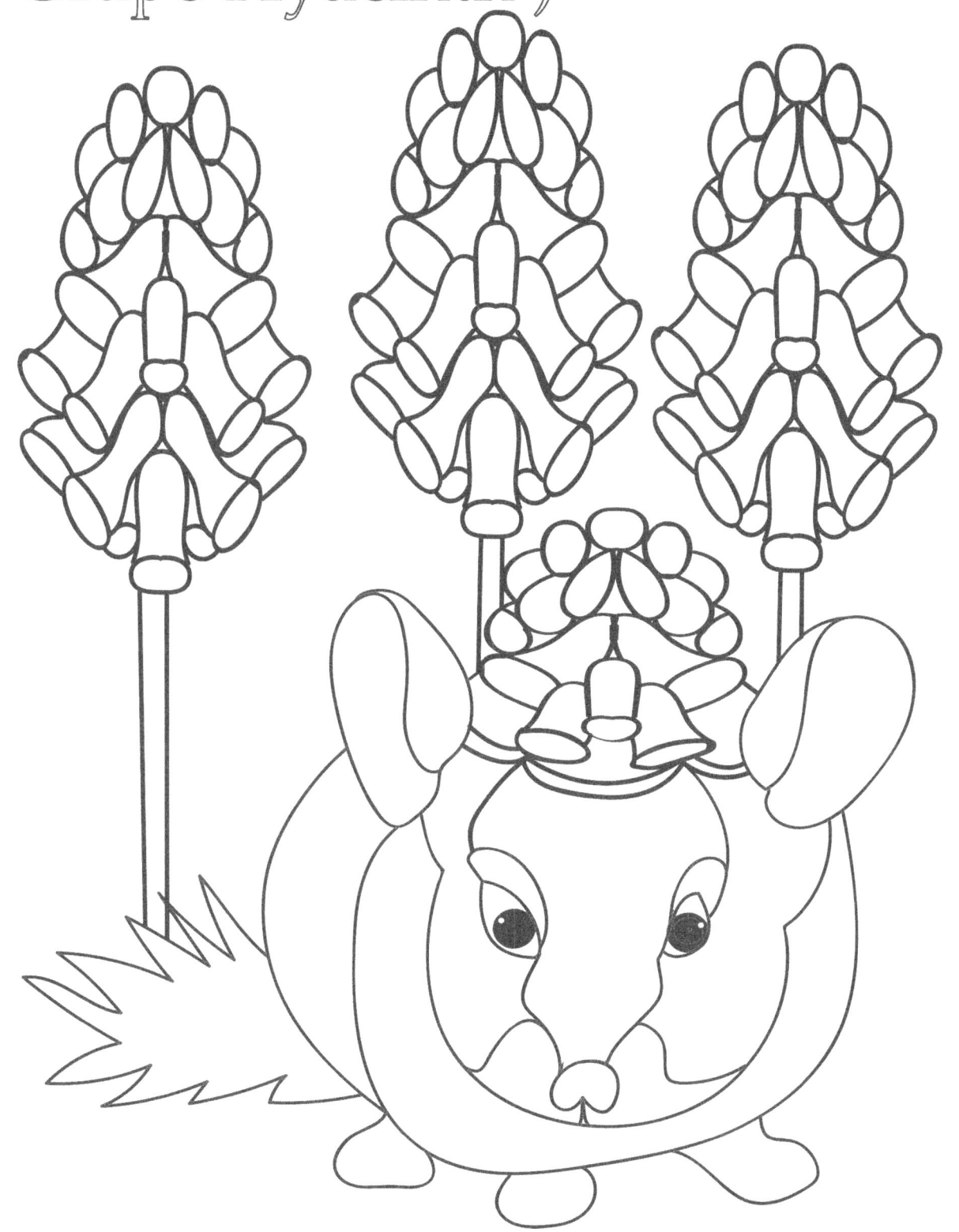

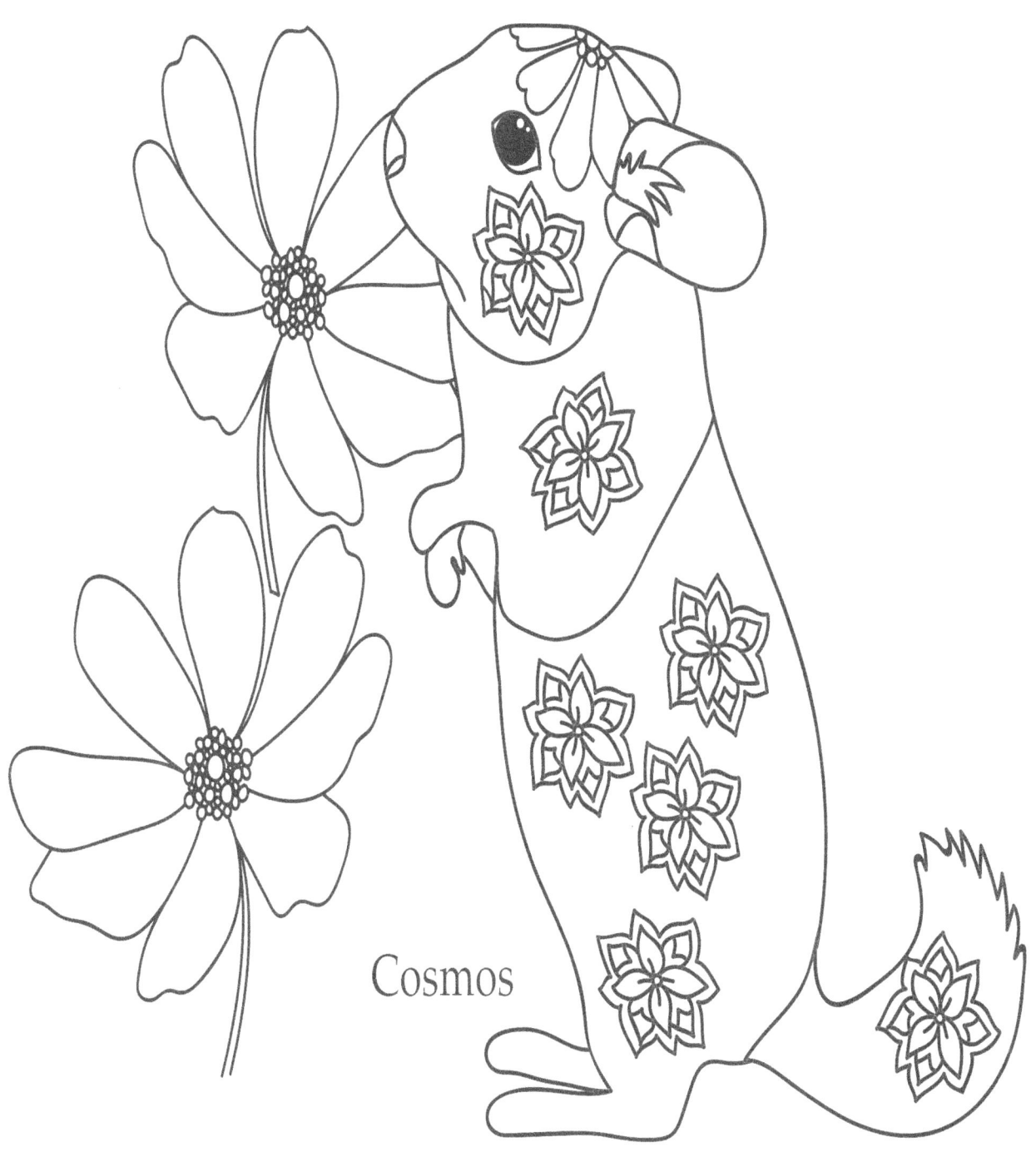
Cosmos

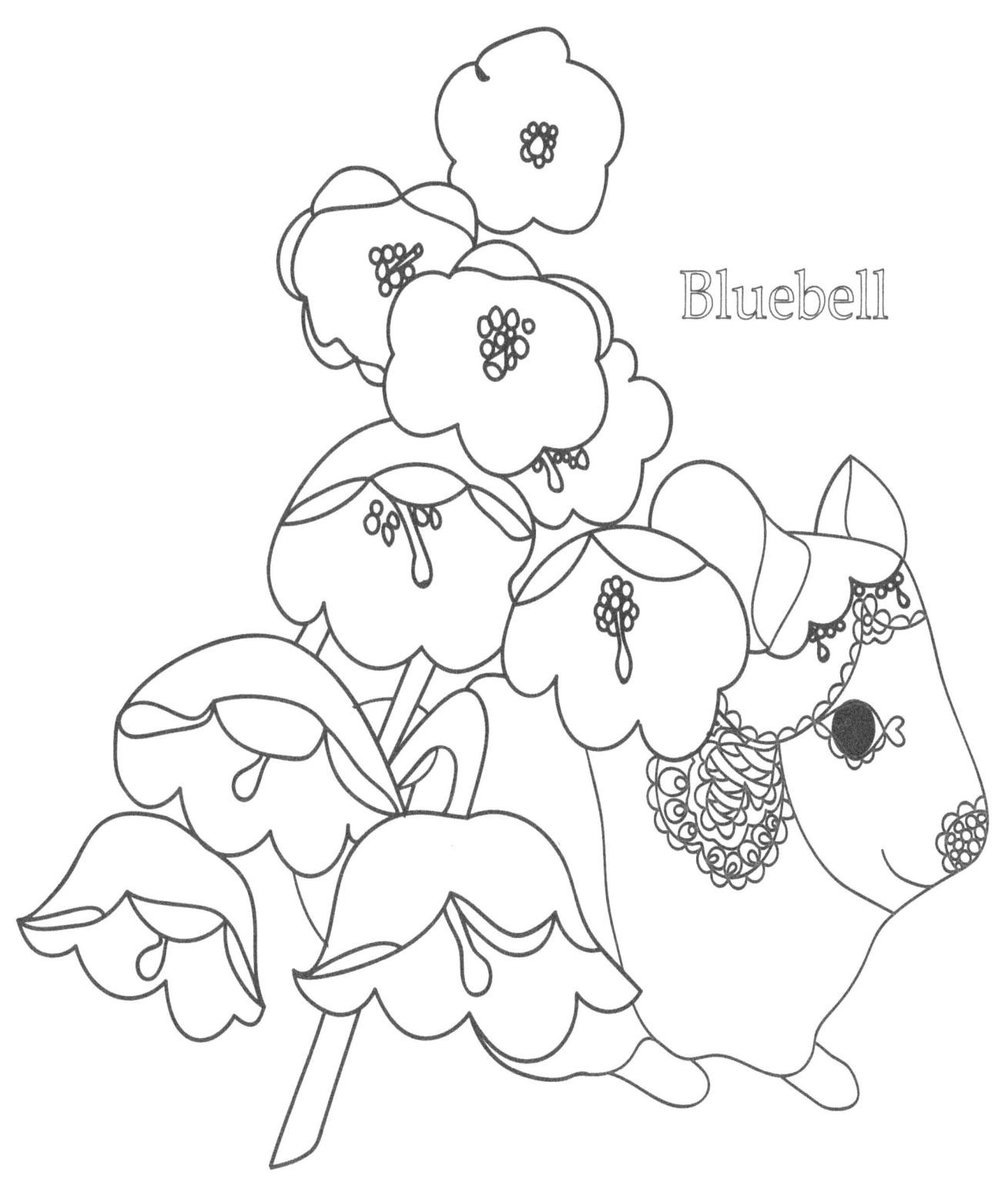

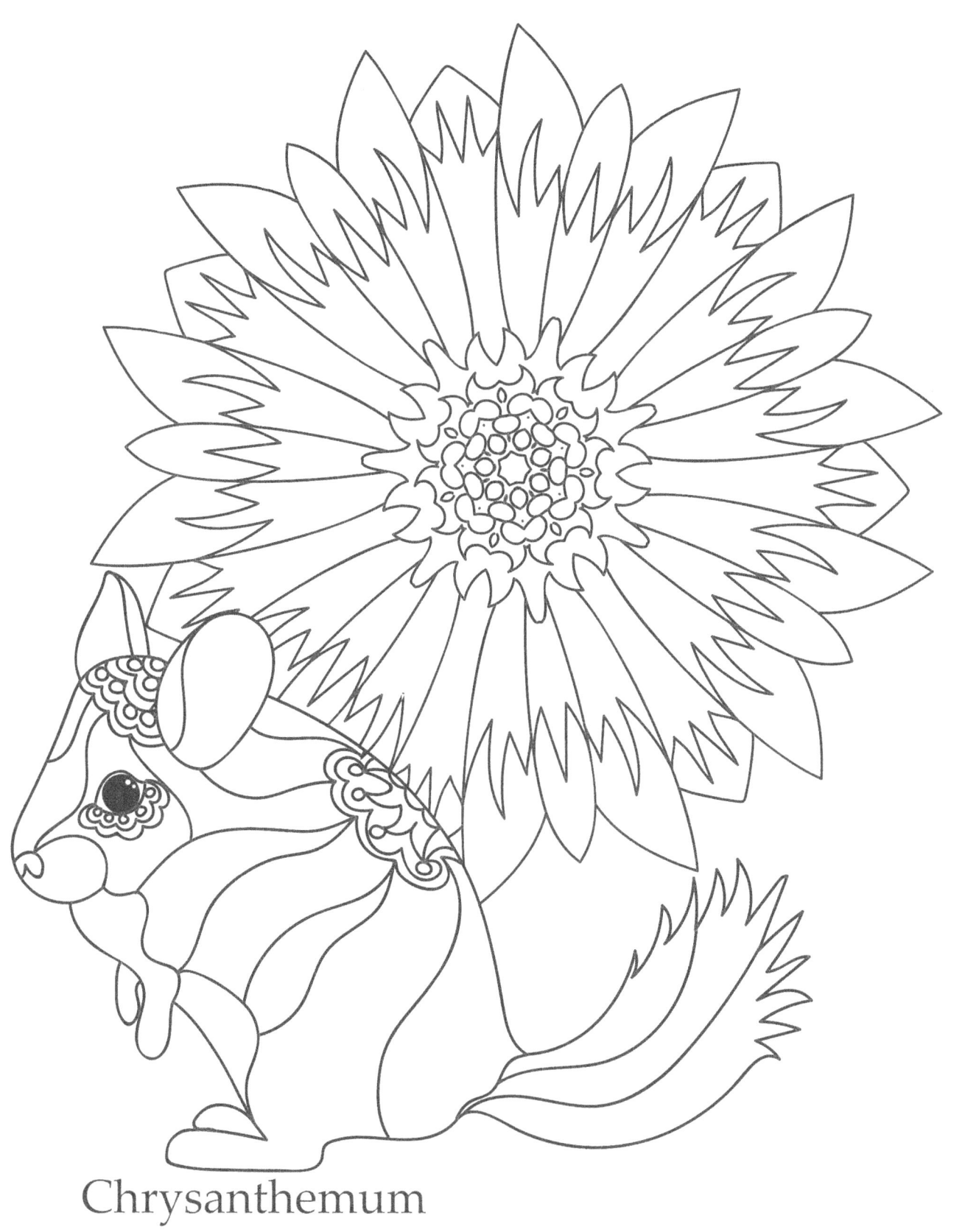
Chrysanthemum

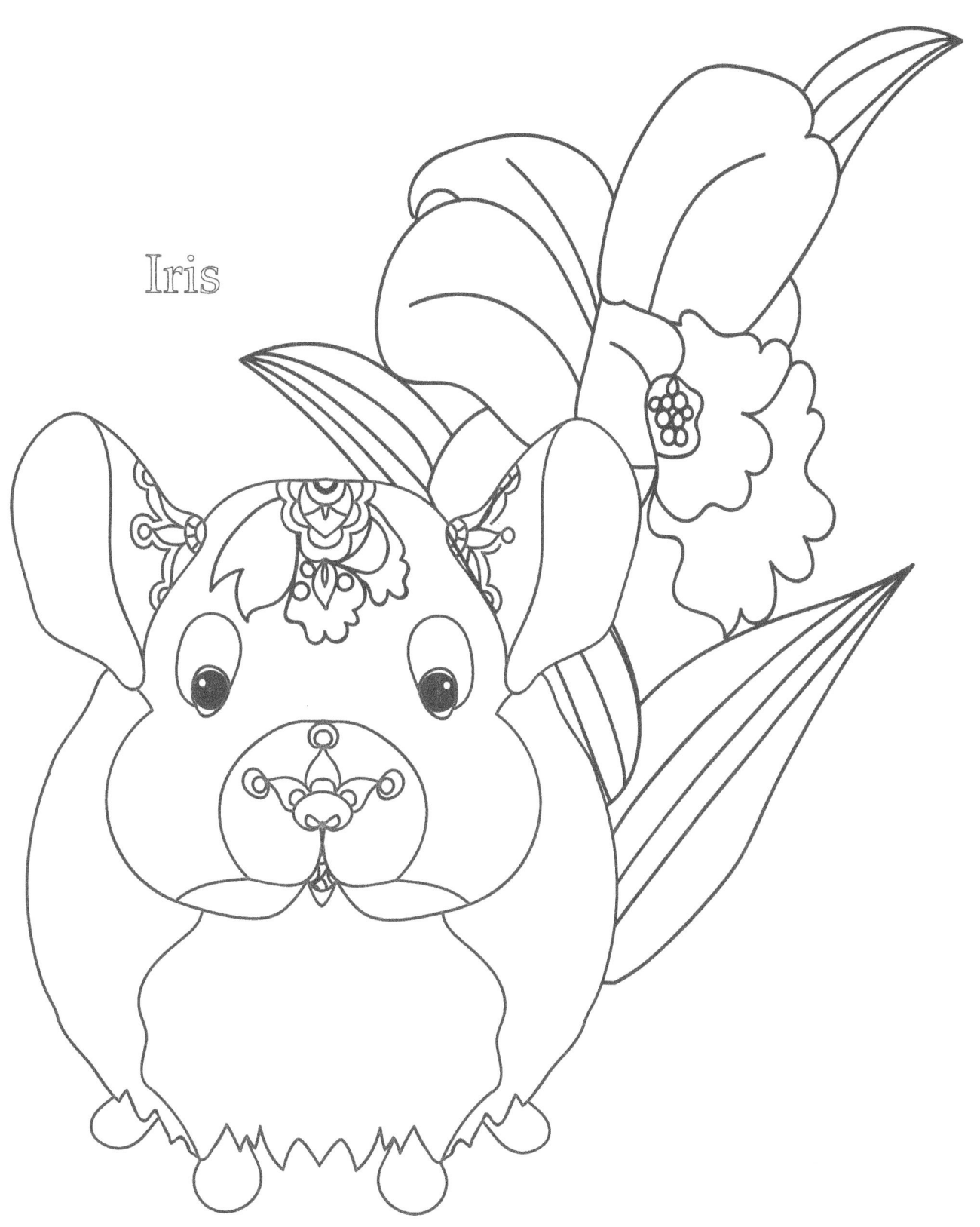

COLOR TEST PAGE

COLOR TEST PAGE